COMING TO AMERICA

THE GERMANS

Jacquelyn Landis, *Book Editor*

Bonnie Szumski, *Publisher*
Helen Cothran, *Managing Editor*

GREENHAVEN PRESS
An imprint of Thomson Gale, a part of The Thomson Corporation

THOMSON
—————★—————™
GALE

Detroit • New York • San Francisco • San Diego • New Haven, Conn.
Waterville, Maine • London • Munich

LIBRARY OF CONGRESS CATALOGING-IN-PUBLICATION DATA
The Germans / Jacquelyn Landis, book editor.
p. cm. — (Coming to America)
Includes bibliographical references and index.
ISBN 0-7377-2152-9 (lib. : alk. paper)
1. German Americans—History. 2. German Americans—History—Sources. 3. Immigrants—United States—History. 4. Germany—Emigration and immigration—History. 5. United States—Emigration and immigration—History. 6. German Americans—Biography. I. Landis, Jacquelyn. II. Coming to America (San Diego, Calif.)
E184.G3G358 2006
973'.0431—dc22   2005051268

CONTENTS

Chapter 3: German Immigration During the 1900s

had to resort to "superpatriotism" to prove their loyalty to America.

ancestors had. Although some German newspapers and clubs still exist, they too have dwindled.

Chapter 4: Notable German Americans

In her popular novels, such as *The Joy Luck Club* and *The Bonesetter's Daughter*, Chinese American author Amy Tan explores the complicated cultural and social differences between Chinese-born mothers and their American-born daughters. For example, the mothers eat foods and hold religious beliefs that their daughters either abhor or abstain from, while the daughters pursue educational and career opportunities that were not available to the previous generation. Generation gaps occur in almost all families, but as Tan's writings show, such differences are even more pronounced when parents grow up in a different country. When immigrants come to the United States, their initial goal is often to start a new life that is an improvement from the life they experienced in their homeland. However, while these newcomers may intend to fully adapt to American culture, they inevitably bring native customs with them. Immigrants have helped make America broader culturally by introducing new religions, languages, foods, and different ways of looking at the world. Their children and subsequent generations, however, often seek to cast aside these traditions and instead more fully absorb mainstream American mores.

As Tan's writings suggest, the dissimilarities between immigrants and their children are manifested in several ways. Adults who come to the United States and do not learn English turn to their children, educated in the American school system, to serve as interpreters and translators. Children, seeing what their American-born schoolmates eat, reject the foods of their native land. Religion is another area where the generation gap is particularly pronounced. For example, the liturgy of Syrian Christian services had to be translated into English when most young Syrian Americans no longer knew how to speak Syriac. Numerous Jews, freed from the European ghettos they had lived in, wished to assimilate more fully into the surrounding culture and began to loosen the traditional dietary and ritual requirements under which they had grown up. Reformed Judaism, which began in Germany, thus found a strong foothold among young Jews born in America.

However, no generational experiences have been as significant as that between immigrant mothers and their daughters. Living in the United States has afforded girls and young women opportunities they likely would not have had in their homelands. The daughters of immigrants, in some cases, live entirely different lives than their mothers did in their native nations. Where an Arab mother may have only received a limited education, her American-raised daughter enjoys a full course of American public schooling, often continuing on to college and careers. A woman raised in India might have been placed in an arranged marriage, while her daughter will have the opportunity to date and choose a husband. Admittedly, not all families have been willing to give their daughters all these new freedoms, but these American-born girls are frequently more willing to declare their wishes.

The generation gap is only one aspect of the immigrant experience in the United States. Understanding immigrants' unique and shared experiences and their contributions to American life is an interesting way to study the many people who make up the American citizenry. Greenhaven Press's Coming to America series helps readers learn why more people have moved to the United States than to any other nation. Selections on the lives of immigrants once they have reached America, from their struggles to find employment to their experiences with discrimination and prejudice, help give students insights into stereotypes and cultural mores that continue to this day. Finally, profiles of prominent immigrants help the reader become aware of the many achievements of these people in fields ranging from science to politics to sports.

Each volume in the Coming to America series takes an extensive look into a particular immigrant population. The carefully selected primary and secondary sources provide both historical perspectives and firsthand insights into the immigrant experience. Combined with an in-depth introduction and a comprehensive chronology and bibliography, every book in the series is a valuable addition to the study of American history. With immigrants comprising nearly 12 percent of the U.S. population, and their children and grandchildren constantly adding to the population, the immigrant experience continues to evolve. Coming to America is consequently a beneficial tool for not only understanding America's past but also its future.

INTRODUCTION

Throughout nearly four hundred years of German immigration, beginning with the Jamestown settlement in 1608, German Americans have made an indelible mark on American life. The 2000 U.S. census revealed that approximately 43 million people, or 15 percent of the total population, define their primary ancestry as German, making German the most frequently reported ancestry in the country. Because German Americans comprise such a large segment of the U.S. population, it is natural that their culture, traditions, and even their language have become woven into the fabric of American society.

Many people are unaware of the German origins of some of the most familiar American customs and practices. Some of America's most endearing holiday traditions, favorite foods, and common expressions are firmly rooted in German history. Even the U.S. kindergarten system is based wholly on a German invention. The German American contribution to society can be seen in many areas, including business and science, but perhaps nowhere is the influence felt so strongly as in American culture.

The Christmas Tree and Santa Claus

The tradition of putting up a Christmas tree began in Germany in the sixteenth century, when Christians brought trees into their homes and decorated them in celebration of the birth of Jesus. The common belief is that Martin Luther, the sixteenth-century Protestant reformer, was walking home one winter evening and became captivated by the twinkling stars he could see through the treetops. Wanting to re-create the beautiful scene in his home, he brought in an evergreen tree and fastened candles to its branches. The tradition spread to other families, and soon Christmas trees were common in Christian households in Germany.

German immigrants who settled in Pennsylvania in the eighteenth century brought their Christmas traditions with them. They would plan festive celebrations on Christmas Eve and Christmas Day, exchanging gifts and preparing lavish feasts complete with beer, singing, and, of course, a decorated tree. However, the custom was not readily adopted by the English settlers, as writer Don Beaulieu describes:

> Christmas trees were slow to catch on in this country. Early Puritan laws forbade the celebration of Christmas, and it was still outlawed in New England until the mid–19th century. By the end of the century, however, Christmas trees decorated with candles, cookies, and ribbons were a common sight in parlors across the country.[1]

Once the notion disappeared that Christmas was a pagan celebration, other Christians embraced the tradition of the Christmas tree along with other elements of the German-style celebration of the birth of the *Christkindl*, or Christ child.

English settlers had trouble pronouncing *Christkindl*, though, and it eventually came to be pronounced Kris Kringle, also known as Santa Claus. The legend of Santa Claus came to America by way of German immigrants. The feast day of St. Nicholas, a kind and generous fourth-century bishop, has long been celebrated in Germany. When Germans immigrated to America, they continued the tradition of honoring St. Nicholas on December 6. How St. Nicholas became the Santa Claus we're familiar with today is told by Dorothy Hoobler and Thomas Hoobler in *The German American Family Album:*

St. Nicholas, called *Sinterklaas* by Pennsylvania Germans, was known for his generosity, particularly to children. The custom of giving gifts to children on this saint's feast day spread from Europe to America with German immigrants. Frequently, men put on false beards and bishops' hats to distribute the gifts. In the 1880s, the German American cartoonist Thomas Nast first drew the image of the fat, jolly, white-bearded man in red who is today's Santa Claus. In this form St. Nicholas became jolly old St. Nick.[2]

After the Protestant Reformation in the sixteenth century, German Protestants also began celebrating the feast day of *Christkindl* on December 25. Reluctant to give up such a beloved hero as St. Nicholas, the two celebrations were combined into one, to be held on December 25. The mingling of the two events was sealed when Christmas celebrations became part of American tradition. Even though the concept of Santa Claus has been thoroughly Americanized, its origins are distinctly German. And even though some modern Christmas trees bear little resemblance to the original evergreen tree festooned with candles, this tradition too is a cultural gift from early German Americans.

The Easter Bunny

Another American holiday that has been shaped by German immigrants is Easter. Most American children look forward to the annual appearance of the Easter bunny. In ancient times, rabbits and hares were recognized as symbols of fertility and were directly associated with pagan festivals of springtime renewal. During the Middle Ages, the Easter hare became part of German culture. The hare delivered eggs and candy to a straw nest placed in a secluded area of the house or garden on the eve of Easter. German immigrants who came to the United States during the eighteenth century and settled in the Pennsylvania Dutch country kept the tradition alive.

As Easter approached, German American children would build nests in the barn or garden, believing that if they were good, the Easter hare, or bunny, would lay colored eggs for them. The nests were made from straw or a boy's cap or girl's bonnet. On Easter Sunday the children would retrieve their nests, and with luck they would be filled with the colored eggs that their parents had surreptitiously placed in them. Soon non-German children began to catch on to the Easter tradition, and the annual arrival of the *Osterhase* (Easter bunny) was a child's greatest pleasure next to the Christmas visit of Kris Kringle.

Even modern chocolate and candy Easter eggs have roots in German culture. The first edible Easter bunnies and treats were made in Germany in the early 1800s. They were usually made of pastry dusted with sugar. These sweet treats, in addition to colored eggs, were given to good children. After more than two centuries of Americanization, the Easter bunny custom has not changed much. Children today receive baskets filled with candy and colored eggs, ostensibly delivered in the night by the Easter bunny. The most modern twist is the Easter egg hunt in which children search for hidden eggs, either real or plastic ones filled with candy. But the tradition remains rooted in the German springtime custom of an egg-delivering Easter bunny.

Oktoberfest

A cherished custom in Germany, the celebration of *Oktoberfest* has been preserved by German Americans and has gradually been adopted by many non-Germans as an annual kickoff to the fall season. The original *Oktoberfest* was a public celebration of the wedding of Crown Prince Ludwig and Princess Therese of Saxony-Hildburghausen, who were married in Munich in 1810. The five-day party was held in a meadow and featured a horse race to mark the close of the event. Over the years the focus gradually shifted to food, beer, music, and dancing as the festival became an annual celebration.

Now, nearly two hundred years later, the party itself remains much the same (minus the horse racing). Susan Spungen, in *Lifetime* magazine, describes the Americanized version:

> Take one warm autumn night, with just a touch of crispness in the air. Add the enticing smells of sizzling sausages, sautéed onions and strong amber beer, stir in the spirited sounds of friends raising a glass to fall. It's a surefire recipe for a perfect . . . Oktoberfest, a spin on the annual two-week party that Germans have been celebrating for 200 years. What started as a royal wedding celebration evolved into a harvest festival wherein one drank to the new beer of fall with what was left of the old beer of winter. What a wonderful excuse for a party.[3]

Although the original *Oktoberfest* was held in October, over the years the festival was moved up to begin in mid-September to avoid the chill that tends to arrive in Germany by October. This is a tradition that is honored in America—most *Oktoberfest* celebrations begin in mid-September and span a period of up to sixteen days. The popularity of *Oktoberfest* seems to increase every year in the United States, and many communities vie to stage a festival even more elaborate than the one held in Munich. Lucy Saunders compares the *Oktoberfest* celebrations in Munich and Cincinnati, which now claims to hold the largest in North America:

> Now, it's Munich vs. Cincinnati, vying for the title of the world's largest Oktoberfest. In Munich, close to a million people show up to consume 10 million pints of beer, some 750,000 spit-roasted chickens, and more than 800,000 wursts and sausages. (Sadly, traditional oom-pah bands are slowly being replaced by taped music—one disgruntled festgoer complained about hearing "La Macarena" more than 200 times during [one] fest in Mu-

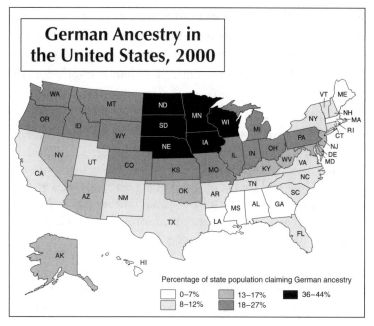

German Ancestry in the United States, 2000

Percentage of state population claiming German ancestry

☐ 0–7%	▨ 13–17%
☐ 8–12%	▨ 18–27%
	■ 36–44%

nich.) In Cincinnati, close to 700,000 people jam the streets of "Zinzinnati" during late September, jostling to music from seven large entertainment stages, while dozens of food vendors serve bratwurst, sauerkraut and thousands of gallons of beer.[4]

The festival is a perfect opportunity for German Americans to celebrate their heritage. It is probable that, more than any other German tradition, *Oktoberfest* is identified by most Americans as being uniquely German.

German American Influence on Food

Like the bratwurst served at *Oktoberfest* celebrations, some foods can be instantly identified as having German origins: sauerkraut, Wiener schnitzel, and perhaps even Black Forest cake. Nonetheless, many Americans are surprised by the everyday foods that have come directly from German American immigrants. For instance, the all-American hamburger derives its name from Hamburg, Germany, and was introduced to Americans in 1904 by German Americans who had settled in St. Louis, Missouri. French fries, an essential accompaniment to hamburgers, would not be the same without ketchup, which was created by German American Henry Heinz in 1892. The hamburger's cousin, the hot dog, also has German American origins:

> Then there's the classic "hot dog," whose main component, the frankfurter, not surprisingly gets its name from the German city of Frankfurt. The frankfurter's history dates back to 1484, and the first hot dog sausages were reportedly sold from a pushcart along with milk rolls and sauerkraut in the 1860s by German immigrants in New York. Meanwhile in St. Louis another German immigrant, Antonoine Feuchtwanger, is said to have invented the sausage in a bun as a way of preventing his customers from being burned by the hot sausages. And it was yet another German immigrant, Charles Feltmann, that opened the first hot dog stand in Coney Island in 1900.[5]

One food having German origins that would surprise many Americans is chili powder. Many German Americans settled in Texas, especially in the community of New Braunfels. There they were exposed to a new style of cooking, one that included smoked meats and spicy sauces and gravies. German immigrants made a contribution to Tex-Mex cuisine that remains an essential ingredient today, as described in *German American Life: Recipes and Traditions:*

> Lovers of Tex-Mex food have a German to thank for the perfect combination of spices, with extracted and ground pulp from the chili pod, that gives their favorite dishes the right taste. Born in Germany, William Gebhart came to the United States, and in 1892 opened a café in the back of Miller's Saloon in New Braunfels, Texas. He soon discovered that the German community loved chili, but couldn't make it until the season of the home-grown chilies. In 1894 he developed the first commercial chili powder by running pepper bits through a small home meat grinder. Two years later Gebhart and Albert Kronkosky opened a factory in San Antonio for the production of chili powder.[6]

Despite the millions of hamburgers, hot dogs, and bowls of chili consumed each year in America, beer may well be the most notable German American culinary contribution. German immigrants were instrumental in establishing breweries, and by the 1850s breweries and beer gardens were commonplace throughout the Eastern states. Although Prohibition made the production of beer (or any other alcoholic beverage) illegal in 1920, beer became popular again when Prohibition was repealed in 1933. Even during Prohibition, "near beer," a beer with a very low alcohol content, was produced in an attempt to satisfy the public's thirst for the beverage.

American dietary habits might be much different today if not for the German American influence on food in the United States. It is hard to imagine a fast food outlet without a hamburger or a major sporting event not offering hot dogs and beer.

The German Influence on Language

Along with customs and traditions, of course, German immigrants brought their own language with them when they came to America. Since large numbers of early German Americans settled in certain locations, particularly in Pennsylvania, Missouri, Virginia, and Ohio, the German language was heard almost as often as English in these places. A persistent myth is that a vote came before Congress in 1795 to make German the official language of the United States, failing by one vote. While this belief is unfounded, Congress did consider printing federal laws in German. In his essay "The Legendary English-Only Vote of 1795," Dennis Barron explains:

> On January 13, 1795, Congress considered a proposal, not to give German any official status, but merely to print the federal laws in German as well as English. During the debate, a motion to adjourn failed by one vote. The final vote rejecting the translation of federal laws, which took place

one month later, is not recorded. The translation proposal itself originated as a petition to Congress on March 20, 1794, from a group of Germans living in Augusta, Virginia. A House committee responding to that petition recommended publishing sets of the federal statutes in English and distributing them to the states, together with the publication of three thousand sets of laws in German.[7]

The subject of translating federal laws into German was debated in Congress several times, with proponents arguing that German Americans who had not yet learned English had a clear disadvantage in understanding the laws of their adopted country. But opponents countered that it had never been the custom in England to translate the laws into Welsh or Gaelic even though many people in Wales or Scotland could not understand English. Many opponents displayed open hostility to the German language. Those opposed to German translations prevailed, but the fact that the issue was seriously considered by Congress shows how predominant the German language was during the early formation of the United States.

Although most German immigrants were eager to learn English, they did not abandon the German language. Eventually, dozens of German words worked their way into the English vocabulary, so much so that some are barely recognizable as being of German origin. The word "blitz," which in German means "lightning," is now commonly used to describe a play in football in which defensive linebackers rush the passer. And the local deli takes its name from the German *Delikatessen*, literally, "delicacies." One word that is more recognizable as German, but still has been thoroughly incorporated into American English, is "gesundheit," which people say when someone sneezes. Most people think the literal translation is "bless you." The word actually means "healthiness," but the usage in German is often the same: to wish good health to someone who has sneezed. "Glitz" and "kitsch" are similar words transplanted from German, the former meaning "extravagant showiness" and the latter "gaudy trash."

German words have filtered into the food we eat as well. The aforementioned hamburgers and frankfurters are two examples, but there are more. Many people enjoy a bowl of *Müsli*, or granola, for breakfast, and the candy Pez, which is dispensed from a rectangular plastic container topped with a popular character's head, is short for *Pfefferminz* (peppermint). The salty pretzels that go so well with beer come directly from the German word *Brezel*. Our noodles are from the German *Nudel*. And the hard, dry zwieback bread that is often fed to teething babies is literally translated as "twice-baked."

We "schlep" things around when we laboriously drag items from one place to another. In fact, a laptop computer in German has the humorous name of *Schlepptop*. Those who enjoy snow skiing are intimately familiar with a "sitzmark," the depression left in the snow after falling backward. Anyone who has had to endure a lengthy and voluble sales pitch can thank the German language for the "spiel." And many people are struck with a case of "wanderlust," or a strong longing to travel.

Finally, there is a special word that is popping up frequently these days, especially in relation to politics. In a time when political divisions in America seem increasingly profound, the word "schadenfreude" is often tossed about on political talk shows. It means "to take delight in another's misfortune," and it is an ideal word to describe the glee with which one side enjoys the other's political setbacks. Its use is quickly spreading to situations outside of politics, too.

Kindergartens and Gymnasiums

In addition to shaping language, German Americans also influenced education. The first kindergarten was established in 1837 in Germany by Friedrich Froebel, who believed that in order to learn, children needed to first develop their social skills by playing and interacting with other children. His theory of early education consisted of four elements: free self-activity, creativity, social participation, and motor expression. Highly controversial at first, by the 1870s Froebel's kindergarten was mandatory for children under the age of six throughout the Austro-Hungarian Empire.

In the United States it was a German immigrant who started the first kindergarten, in 1856. Margarethe Schurz, who was the wife of Civil War general and statesman Carl Schurz, was familiar with Froebel's theories when she came to America. A teacher in Germany, Schurz and her family settled in Watertown, Wisconsin, where she taught her daughter and other children of friends and relatives through the use of arts and crafts, music, and play, all according to Froebel's techniques. So many parents prevailed upon Schurz to teach their children that she eventually opened a small kindergarten in which instruction was given in German. In 1859 Elizabeth Peabody, a teacher in Massachusetts who had heard of Froebel's concept, visited Schurz to see for herself this new kind of school. Peabody subsequently opened the first English kindergarten in the United States, in Boston, which was the beginning of an institution that had a sweeping effect on American education.

Another German education concept that was brought to America is that of the gymnasium. In the United States the word "gymnasium" connotes a building where basketball and other indoor sports are played. "Gymnasium," however, is a word that comes from ancient Greece, meaning a place for both the physical and intellectual education of young men. In Germany gymnasiums came to be more focused on secondary schooling to prepare for higher education at a university. Americans, of course, use gymnasiums solely for physical activity.

German Americans' Legacy

In 1983 President Ronald Reagan officially recognized the significance of German immigrants' contributions to American life. He proclaimed October 6 to be German Day in honor of German Americans, and every president since has continued this annual day of recognition. President George W. Bush captured the essence of the German American spirit in his October 3, 2003, proclamation of German American Day:

> As one of the largest ethnic groups in the United States, German Americans have greatly influenced our country in the fields of business, government, law, science, athletics, the arts, and many others. Henry Engelhard Steinway and his sons founded Steinway & Sons in 1853. The 300,000th Steinway piano, the "golden grand," was presented to President Franklin Roosevelt in 1938, and is still on display at the White House. John Augustus Roebling and his son pioneered the development of suspension bridges and wire cable. Their construction of the Brooklyn Bridge is a lasting landmark to their skill, determination, and innovation. And entrepreneurs such as John Davison Rockefeller, John Wanamaker, and Milton Snavely Hershey helped to strengthen the American economy and inspire others to reach for the American Dream. In addition to their many professional achievements, German Americans have influenced American culture. From Christmas trees to kindergartens, the United States has adopted many German traditions and institutions. By celebrating and sharing their customs and traditions, German Americans help to preserve their rich heritage and enhance the cultural diversity of our Nation.[8]

As recognized by U.S. presidents, German Americans have indeed, left a lasting mark on American culture.

Notes

1. Don Beaulieu, "O Christmas Tree," *U.S. Catholic*, December 1995, p. 50.

2. Dorothy Hoobler and Thomas Hoobler, *The German American Family Album*. New York: Oxford University Press, 1996, p. 109.

3. Susan Spungen, "Throw Your Own Oktoberfest," *Lifetime*, October 2004, p. 94.

4. Lucy Saunders, "Oktoberfest!" *Global Gourmet*, June 15, 2005. www.global gourmet.com/food/egg/egg1097/oktoberfest.html.

5. *German Agricultural Marketing Board*, "Old World Roots with a New Twist: Reviewing the 'All-American' Barbecue." www.germanfoods.org/consumer/All-AmericanBarbecuehasGermanroots.cfm.

6. John D. Zug and Karen Gottier, eds., *German American Life: Recipes and Traditions*. Iowa City, IA: Penfield, 1991, pp. 133–34.

7. Dennis Barron, "The Legendary English-Only Vote of 1795," April 10, 2003. www.watzmann.net/scg/german-by-one-vote.html.

8. George W. Bush, "German American Day, 2003," White House Proclamation Archives, October 3, 2003. www.whitehouse.gov/news/releases/2003/10/20031003-11.html.

CHAPTER 1

The First Wave: German Immigration Before 1800

COMING TO AMERICA

The First Germans Arrive in America: Life in Jamestown

Gary C. Grassl

The first German immigrants to arrive in America, in 1608, were part of the original settlement of Jamestown, Virginia. Along with their fellow colonists, they faced brutal hardships while trying to eke out a living and coexist with the natives. In the following selection Gary C. Grassl describes the German immigrants' early days—how their remarkable industriousness set them apart from the other colonists, and how their skills at glassmaking and construction were instrumental in the development of Jamestown. Grassl is a former writer and editor for the *Wall Street Journal*. He is also the former president of the German American Heritage Society of Greater Washington, D.C.

The first seeds of this country were planted at Jamestown, Virginia, the first permanent English settlement in what is today the United States of America. The first English settlers arrived at Jamestown in 1607; the first German, in 1608. Therefore, Germans were present at the creation of this nation. The Germans who came to Jamestown in 1608 and subsequently in 1620 were the forerunners of the largest nationality to immigrate to the United States since its founding in 1776.

The first Germans to reach the Jamestown Colony came

aboard the English vessel *Mary and Margaret* captained
by Christopher Newport. They left England around July
1608 and arrived in Virginia around 1 October—12 years
before the Pilgrims landed in Massachusetts. They consisted of up to five unnamed glassmakers and three carpenters or house builders—Adam, Franz and Samuel. They
came in a group of about 70 new settlers, including several
Polish makers of pitch and tar, soap ashes and potashes.
Jamestown at that time consisted of nothing but a small
wooden fort on a peninsula of the James, a river, which
flows into Chesapeake Bay near modern Norfolk, VA. . . .

The Germans and the Poles faced precarious conditions
at James Fort, which had been built on the north bank of
the James River by June 1607. More than half of the original 105 settlers were already dead by the first autumn.

The German Glassmakers

Captain John Smith, the President of the Jamestown
Colony, complained that most of the settlers were unac-
customed to hard labor. They "never did know what a day's
work was, except the Dutchmen [Germans] and Poles, and
some dozen other." Many were unused to hard labor, because they were gentlemen. The German glassmen and carpenters and Polish pitch, tar and soap-ash makers, who
were recruited from their particular countries because of
their skills, went right to work producing commodities, including clapboard and wainscot plus "a trial of glass" to
send back with Newport's ship around 1 December 1608.
This first sample of glass was made at James Fort where
Hessian crucibles with adhering glass were discovered by
archaeologists.

After their initial experimenting with glass production
within the Fort, the German glassmakers built a Glasshouse probably with the help of the German carpenters
and others. Like James Fort, it faced the James River,

which provided a ready supply of sand for glassmaking. The Glasshouse was located on the mainland, however, just beyond the narrow strip of land that connected it to the peninsula on which stood James Fort. It was described in a contemporaneous account as situated "in the woods near a mile from James Town." Its distance from the Fort exposed it to Indian attack, but its bordering forest provided the fuel for firing its glass furnaces and kiln. In fact, the reason the English wanted to establish a glasshouse in distant Virginia in the first place was because firewood was as abundant there as it was scarce at home. The colonists' secretary William Strachey described it in 1610 as "a goodly house . . . with all offices and furnaces thereto belonging."

The Glasshouse accommodated three ovens made of river boulders cemented together with clay: A fritting furnace for preheating the glass ingredients, a working furnace for melting the glass and for keeping it at working temperature, and an annealing furnace for slowly cooling the finished pieces. The Glasshouse, which measured about 37 by 50 feet, also included a kiln to fire pots or crucibles used in melting the glass. . . .

In 1609, the Glasshouse went into full production. According to [archeologist Jean Carl] Harrington, "Archeological evidence [shows] that considerable glass was melted and fabricated. It shows also that all of it was 'common green' glass." This was known as *Waldglas* in Germany. There is no documentation of glass production after 1609. "In any event, glassmaking most certainly would not have continued during the terrible period of starvation and sickness" during the winter of 1609–10 when "all but 60 of the 500 inhabitants of Jamestown died," writes Harrington. "Relief came to the Colony in the spring of 1610, but there is no evidence that the glass factory was revived at the time." We don't know if the operation ceased because of the poor quality of the sand from the James River

. . . , the difficulty and cost of transporting such a breakable product such a long distance, or if the German glassmakers died during the winter of 1609–10 along with the majority of settlers.

After investigating the remains of the Glasshouse, Harrington concludes that "the colonists made a sincere attempt to start a manufacturing enterprise, and that even though the time was not ripe for success in their glass ventures, they were able to, and did, produce a workable glass comparable to that made in English glass houses."

Hardships Faced by the First Germans

The story of the Jamestown Colony's first years is one of incredible hardships, failures, dissension, and premature death. It seems almost a miracle today that the settlement survived. The pioneer Germans were caught up in the same dire straits as their English companions, and they shared a similar fate. The settlers, few of whom were farmers or fishermen, were constantly short of food. Instead of first becoming self sufficient, the settlers were forced to spend time and energy in searching for precious metals or in producing products that might turn a profit for the parent company in London.

The English traded copper and casting counters, among other things, for Indian corn. The copper, which the natives valued highly, came from the German-run and staffed Society of the Mines Royal headquartered in Keswick, England; it held the monopoly on the production of this metal in England. The brass-like casting counters or *Rechenpfennig*, many of which are still being found around Jamestown by archaeologists, bear their maker's names, such as Hans Laufer, Hans Krauwinkel and Hans Schultes zu Nürnberg; some bear such German inscriptions as *Gotes Reich Bleibt Ewick* (God's Kingdom Endures Forever).

The natives were accustomed to growing just enough corn to meet their annual needs; therefore, they had little surplus. When they refused to trade any more corn with the settlers, Smith forced them to hand over their supplies or see their villages burned.

In December 1608, Powhatan, the chief of the neighboring tribes, promised to provide Smith with corn if he would send him guns, swords, and an English coach in addition to building him a European-style house. At this point, Smith decided to send the German house builders to Powhatan.

The German Carpenters

Smith sent him Adam, Franz, and Samuel, who had arrived around October 1608 with the German glassmakers. (Powhatan is probably best known popularly today as the father of Pocahontas.) Smith was willing to send the house builders to the Indian chief, because he didn't have enough food for them to sustain their labor at Jamestown. But above all he wanted to use the substantial house they would build as a "castle," as he said, for trapping and killing Powhatan and as a subsequent refuge for himself, explains the American historian Conway Whittle Sams. This intended murder of Powhatan, however, was in direct defiance of orders from the Virginia Company of London to treat the native chief kindly. Smith tells us that he specifically instructed one of the Germans—Samuel—to spy on Powhatan so that he could get the chief in his grasp.

Smith sent the three German carpenters and some Englishmen by a direct overland route northward from James Fort about 13 miles to Powhatan's chief village. Werowocomoco was located on the north bank of what the English called the York River. It was situated near today's Purtan Bay, a corruption of Powhatan Bay. Here the carpenters began to construct one of the first substantial European-style houses in English America.

Meanwhile on 29 December 1608, Smith set out also for Werowocomoco with 46 armed men. But instead of going overland, he went in two small ships down the James and then up the York River. He arrived at the chief's headquarters on 12 January 1609.

When several of the leaders left behind at Jamestown became aware of Smith's intention to kill Powhatan, they tried to avert his misdeed by following after him. Their vessel sank, however, in a squall, and all eleven drowned.

False Accusations of the Germans

Smith was unsuccessful in his attempt to kill the chief. "Of course Smith claimed his failure to kill Powhatan was not his fault," writes Sams. "We all love to blame some one else for our failures; and so Smith blames the Dutchmen for his failure. They had told Powhatan his plans; and the trap which he was laying in the house they were to build for Powhatan, did not work." Nevertheless, Smith left the Germans behind to finish the chief's house.

Powhatan must have realized that Adam, Franz and Samuel were bound by a special bond; perhaps he concluded from their distinctive language that they belonged to a different tribe from the English. Powhatan took advantage of this knowledge.

After Smith's departure, the chief forced two of the German carpenters, Adam and Franz, "two stout Dutchmen," to walk the 13 miles overland to James Fort before Smith could get back there with his ships. This was easily accomplished, because the ships had to travel the roundabout way down the York and back up the James. Powhatan ordered the two Germans to ask for another set of arms and tools under the pretext that theirs were needed by Smith. Powhatan forced them to bring back these weapons by holding their compatriot Samuel as hostage.

In the words of Smith, "Samuel their other consort Powhatan kept for their pledge."

American historians have condemned Adam and Franz for betraying the English by delivering two muskets and two swords to the Indians. But they had little choice: Smith had placed them between a rock and a hard place. Besides, many English settlers also conveyed weapons to the Indians. Smith said that a total of 300 hatchets, 50 swords, 8 guns and 8 pikes were delivered to the natives at this time.

Smith blamed all this also on the Germans. According to Smith, the German carpenters persuaded many Englishmen to arm Powhatan in order to destroy the English Colony. He would have us believe that these carpenters, who knew little English, were so eloquent and crafty that they could persuade a sizable number of English settlers to make common cause with the people they considered "savages" in order to destroy their own kind.

A more likely explanation is that the starving English were trading their tools and weapons for food. But Smith couldn't admit that conditions were so bad under his governorship that his men were forced to barter away their weapons to stay alive. So he invented a grand conspiracy organized by three German carpenters.

Meanwhile, the Germans lived in Powhatan's household, which included his daughter Pocahontas. The carpenters finished Powhatan's house, "in which he took such pleasure, especially in the lock and key, which he so admired, as locking and unlocking his door a hundred times a day, he thought no device in the world comparable to it."

Smith Terrorized the Countryside

Smith tried to kill Powhatan a second time, but when the captain arrived in Werowocomoco, he discovered that the chief had fled from the house the Germans had built for him. Smith again blamed the Germans for the chief's escape. He complained, "those damned Dutchmen had caused Powhatan to abandon his new house and Werowocomoco and to carry away all his corn and provision." But in fact Powhatan didn't need to be prompted by anyone to get away the moment his scouts told him Smith was coming. Wherever Smith went, he terrorized the countryside and forced the natives to hand over their corn.

George Percy, who would succeed Smith as chief executive of the Colony, characterized him as "an ambitious, unworthy and vainglorious fellow." Percy wrote that Smith "stuffed" his reports about what occurred at Jamestown with "many falsities" and "malicious distractions. . . ." The American historian Alexander Brown thinks that Smith and the historians who relied on him did "great injustice" to "the men who gave their time, their talents, and their lives to establishing the first Protestant colony in our country."

Some time after Smith had returned to Jamestown from his second attempt to kill Powhatan, the German carpenter Franz, "a stout young fellow," appeared at the Glasshouse. Smith charged him with being up to no good because he was "disguised like a savage." The truth is that Franz simply looked like a native after having lived among them; certain Englishmen who had also lived among the Indians were later described as also having taken on an Indian appearance.

Smith sent 20 musketeers after Franz, who in the face of such a force retreated back into the woods. But he was captured, according to Smith. Franz himself said that he came voluntarily to Jamestown. He "extremely complained" that Powhatan had "detained them per force." Franz declared that he had "made this escape with the hazard of his life." He explained that "to save their lives they were constrained" by Powhatan to supply him with arms. Nevertheless Smith put Franz in shackles, and he sent [a] message to Powhatan to return the remaining two Germans. Powhatan replied, however, that "the Dutchmen would not return, neither did Powhatan stay them; and to bring them fifty miles on his men's backs they were not able." Powhatan was having his little joke with Smith; the chief had his reasons for detaining the Germans.

Smith Is Sent Back to England

Meanwhile, from about February to May 1609, a good deal of work was being done in and about James Fort, including the construction of "some twenty houses, and "a blockhouse in the neck of our isle" as protection. Since Franz was in Jamestown during part of this period, he would have participated in this building work.

In the summer of 1609 Smith got it into his head that Adam, Samuel "and one Bentley another fugitive" planned "to destroy the colony" in the service of Spain. This was a notion worthy of a science fiction writer. He sent "William Volday, a Zwitzar [Swiss] by birth," after them. But instead of bringing them back, the Swiss German, "this double villain". . ."this wicked hypocrite" joined "his cursed countrymen . . . to effect their projects. . . ." Smith then engaged two Englishmen "to go and stab them or shoot them." But when they reached the Germans, they decided against carrying out Smith's orders.

Powhatan then released Adam, but Samuel stayed behind. Adam and Volday then rejoined the Jamestown settlers without being punished, which shows that Smith's notion about their "villainy" was not shared by the rest of the colonists. As a matter of fact, when the colonists later arrested Smith and sent him back to England to face charges, one of these was that he had tried to kill the Germans who were with Powhatan.

Then we read this curious sentence in Smith's chronicle: "but Samuel still stayed with Powhatan to hear further of their estates by this supply." In other words, Smith kept

Samuel with Powhatan to report to the captain about what the Indians were doing. This is curious indeed! First Smith wanted to have Samuel killed, because he allegedly sought to destroy the Colony. But a short while later, Smith decided to continue to keep Samuel as his personal agent with Powhatan so that he could ferret out the chief's plans. What a strange metamorphosis! One moment Samuel is so evil that he must be killed; a short while later, he is so trustworthy that he can be employed as Smith's personal operative.

In October 1609, Smith was shipped back to England a prisoner to face a number of charges, including having plotted to kill the German carpenters.

A Disastrous Escape

Late in 1609, while Samuel remained with Powhatan, the Indian Chief ambushed an English party of about 30 under Captain Ratcliffe whom he had invited to trade copper for corn. First Powhatan welcomed Ratcliffe to his village of Pamunkey and brought along Samuel and two Englishmen, Spelman and Savage, who were also staying with the Indians. This village was located near modern West Point [site of the U.S. military academy] at the tip of the peninsula formed by the confluence of the Pamunkey and Mattaponi Rivers. Powhatan let Samuel and the Englishmen stay with Ratcliffe that night. The next day, when the trading was going on, a dispute arose between the English and the Indians. Powhatan left the scene and took Samuel with him. A war party hiding in the woods then killed almost all of Ratcliffe's men.

Henry Spelman, one of the two Englishmen with Powhatan, tells us what happened next: "Now, while this business was in action, the Powhatan sends me and one Samuel, a Dutchman, to a town about sixteen miles off, called Yawtanoone, willing us there to stay for him. . . . "The King [Powhatan], in show, made still much of us; yet

his mind was much declined from us, which made us fear
the worst. And, having now been with him about twenty-
four or twenty-five weeks, it happened that the King [chief]
of [the] Potomac [tribe] came to visit the great Powhatan,
where, being a while with him, he showed such kindness
to Savage, Samuel and myself, as we determined to go away
with him.

"When the day of his departure was come, we did as we
agreed, and having gone a mile or two on the way, Savage
feigned some excuse of stay; and, unknown to us went
back to the Powhatan, and acquainted him with our de-
parting with the Potomac.

"The Powhatan presently sends after us, commanding
our return, which we refusing, went still on our way; and
those that were sent went still on with us, till one of them,
finding opportunity, on a sudden, struck Samuel with an
ax, and killed him . . ." thus died the German house builder
Samuel while trying to escape from chief Powhatan.

The "Starving Time"

"The winter of 1609–10 has been described through the
years as the 'starving time,' seemingly, an accurate description," writes the American historian Charles E. Hatch, Jr.
It saw the population shrink to about 12 percent "as a result of disease, sickness, Indian arrows, and malnutrition."

"So lamentable was our scarcity that we were constrained to eat dogs, cats, rats, snakes, toadstools, horse-
hides and what not," wrote a contemporary. "One man, out
of the misery he endured, killing his wife powdered
[salted] her up to eat her, for which he was burned. Many
besides fed on the corpses of dead men. . . ."

During the "starving time," Adam and Franz returned
to Powhatan, the alternative being death by starvation or
disease. They may not have known that Samuel had been
killed.

After the starving time, the English decided to abandon the settlement. "On June 7, 1610, the settlers, except some of the Poles and Dutchmen who were with Powhatan, boarded their ship and started down the James," writes Hatch.

"The next morning, while still in the river, advance word reached [them] that Lord Delaware had arrived at Point Comfort on the way to Jamestown and was bringing 150 settlers and a generous supply. . . . On June 10, Delaware reached 'James Citty' and made his landing. . . . With the arrival of Delaware, the settlement was given new life and new hope."

The Swiss German Volday [or Waldi], who had gone back to England with Captain Samuel Argall in 1609 to report to the Company, returned with Lord Delaware to resume prospecting for minerals. Volday, however, died of a disease, as did the majority of the early settlers. Delaware himself took sick.

When the German carpenters Adam and Franz heard that the English were re-establishing their settlement, they tried to rejoin them, but Powhatan "caused his men to beat out their brains," states a contemporary report. The fact that the two German carpenters were killed trying to get away from Powhatan is surely proof that they were not collaborators. . . .

The Importance of the Germans at Jamestown

When we commemorate the first Germans at Jamestown, we must not exaggerate the importance of these few men to the physical survival of the first permanent English Colony. Their assigned task of producing glass as a profitable product proved impractical; nevertheless, they produced the first "industrial" commodity in English America. The remains of their furnaces constitute the oldest existing structure in English America, the only one harking back to the earliest years of Jamestown. The house builders were placed in an untenable position by Captain Smith when he sent them to the Indians: There they had to serve with unswerving loyalty two implacable enemies— Powhatan and Smith—an impossible task. Nevertheless, they contributed to the construction of Jamestown. . . . The story of the first Germans at Jamestown is the same as that of the first English: Initial failures that laid the groundwork for eventual success. The Germans at Jamestown probably all died without descendants. . . .

The importance of the Germans at Jamestown is that they were among the first settlers of Virginia and English America, that they were valued for their skills, and although small in number, they were representative of the millions more to come. When we remember the first Germans at Jamestown, we can say with pride that Germans took part in the settlement that may be called with more justification than any other the place where the American nation had its beginning. They were thus present at the creation of this nation.

Germantown: The First Permanent German Settlement in America

Don Heinrich Tolzmann

Many religious sects, including the Quakers, were considered illegal in Germany. At the urging of William Penn—a Quaker writer, religious reformer, statesman, and the founder of Pennsylvania—thirteen German Mennonite and Quaker families sailed from Germany in 1683 to establish a permanent settlement in America. In the following selection author Don Heinrich Tolzmann describes the early days of Germantown, the hamlet outside of Philadelphia where the immigrants settled. Tolzmann describes the varied skills the immigrants brought with them and how their industrious and peace-loving nature helped them establish a thriving community. The author is the curator of the German-Americana Collection and director of the German-American Studies Program at the University of Cincinnati. He is also the author of *German-American Achievements: 400 Years of Contributions to America* and *The German-American Experience*, from which this selection is excerpted.

The first permanent German settlement in America was founded in 1683 at Germantown, Pennsylvania, by a group of thirteen German families who had emigrated from Krefeld, Germany. William Penn had been largely instrumental in bringing them to America. Inspired with mis-

Don Heinrich Tolzmann, *The German-American Experience*. Amherst, NY: Humanity Books, 2000. Copyright © 2000 by Don Heinrich Tolzmann. All rights reserved. Reproduced by permission.

sionary zeal, the young Englishman visited the Nether-
lands and Germany in 1671 and 1677 to gain adherents for
the Quaker faith. As early as 1655 George Fox, the founder
of the Society of the Friends [Quakers], had sent messen-
gers to the European continent. When Penn arrived on the
Rhine River, he found a small community of Quakers located near Worms in a village named Kriegsheim.

The Rhineland was at this time fertile ground for the
spreading of Quaker teachings. They stressed the inward
life, spirituality as opposed to dogma, simplicity and pu-
rity of living, and opposition to war and violence. In addition to Quakers there were Mennonites, Schwenkfelders,
Dunkards, and Pietists. Since by German law only the
Catholic, Lutheran, and Reformed Churches were officially
recognized and established, these various sects were considered illegal.

William Penn, who is said to have preached in German,
received a warm and cordial reception when he spoke along
the Rhine and in Frankfurt am Main. Although he made
some converts to Quakerism, Penn's greatest achievement
was not religious, but rather political and social. It was his
appearance on the Rhine that drew attention to the possibility of immigration to America.

Pennsylvania Is Established

In lieu of a payment of sixteen thousand pounds in ster-
ling which the British government owed Admiral Penn, his
son, William, was given a tract of land that became known
as Pennsylvania. Shortly after the issuing of a royal char-
ter, a brief description of the province was published in
1681 by William Penn. Among other things, it pointed out
the advantages for immigrants in Pennsylvania. It also described the favorable location, the fertile soil, and the
wealth in game and fish available. This book was then
translated into German, *Eine Nachricht wegen der Land-*

schaft Pennsylvania in Amerika[1] (Amsterdam: Christoph Conraden, 1681), and it came to the attention of the Pietists in Frankfurt am Main.

The Frankfurters were intrigued by the possibilities of life in the New World, and they formed a company for the purpose of emigration. Through Benjamin Furley, Penn's agent, they purchased fifteen thousand acres of wilderness. Later, the Frankfurt Company, as it was called, extended its holdings to twenty-five thousand acres, offering a share of five thousand acres for one hundred pounds. Although there was much enthusiasm about life in the New World, none of the Frankfurt circle, who apparently were cultured and well-to-do individuals, came to America.

Only their agent, Franz Daniel Pastorius, came to America. He was a well-educated and widely traveled lawyer who became so deeply interested in the project that he decided to cast his lot with the immigrants. According to Pastorius, the discussion of the immigration project "begat a desire in my soul to continue in their society and with them to lead a quiet, godly, and honest life in a howling wilderness." He then sailed from Deal, England, in June 1683, on the ship *America* with a number of men and women of humble origin. While crossing the ocean, Pastorius won the friendship of Welsh physician and Oxford scholar Thomas Lloyd, who later became the president of the Provincial Council. Since Pastorius knew no English at that time and Lloyd was ignorant of German, they both conversed in Latin. Penn was delighted with Pastorius, who landed on August 20, 1683, and gave him a cordial reception. Twice a week the young lawyer dined at the governor's house. Pastorius wrote, "As I was recently absent from home a week, he [Penn] came himself to visit me and bade me dine with him twice every week, and declared to his counsellors that

---

1. German for *A Report on the Area of Pennsylvania in America*

he loved me and the High Germans very much and wished them to so likewise." Penn characterized Pastorius as "sober, upright, wise and pious—a man everywhere esteemed and of unspotted name."

Thirteen Families Settled Germantown

The cultured Pastorius was amused by the poorly built houses of the city of Philadelphia, which had been laid out only two years before and consisted, as he records in his diary, largely of woods and brushwood. He wrote that this made a striking impression on him, especially after having come from London, Paris, Amsterdam, and Ghent.

The first company of actual immigrants from Krefeld, Germany, set out six weeks later on the *Concord*, considered the *Mayflower* of the German immigration, which was commanded by Captain [William] Jeffreys. The devout group of German Mennonites and Quakers consisted of thirteen families, and on October 6, 1683, the vessel landed safely at the port city of Philadelphia. Their arrival is considered the founding date of the first German settlement in America: Germantown, Pennsylvania, which the newcomers established six miles above the city. Originally called *Deutschstadt*, the name was soon changed to Germantown, which was easier for non-Germans to pronounce. In 1987 October 6 was proclaimed "German-American Day" by congressional and presidential proclamation, and has been celebrated annually ever since.

Pastorius had made the arrangements for the immigrants' departure from Kriegsheim and Krefeld, and he also provided for them when they arrived in Philadelphia. The Frankfurt Company had purchased 25,000 acres of land, and the Krefelder settlers 8,000. In his *Grund und Lagerbuch*,[2] Pastorius describes the severe hardships of the early settlers

2. German for "real estate records," this was the first official document of Germantown.

but lauds their "Christian endurance and indefatigable industry." Pastorius shared their difficulties and lived temporarily in a tiny wooden shack with oil-soaked paper for windows, but maintained his humor and his scholarship throughout. Governor Penn laughed heartily when he read the motto the young lawyer had placed over his wretched dwelling: *Parva domus sed amica bonis, procul este profani* (Small is my house, but it welcomes the good people; may the godless ones stay away.) The colonists built small huts, dug cellars, and passed their first winter in much discomfort, but by the next year, better and more permanent dwellings had been constructed, and grain from the first crops (Indian corn and buckwheat) had been stockpiled for the winter.

Settlers Had Valuable Skills

The industries that the settlers had brought from Krefeld stood them in good stead. There were skillful weavers who produced so much that a store was opened in Philadelphia. They laid out vineyards and raised flax. Within a short time a wide variety of tradesmen, including carpenters, locksmiths, shoemakers, and tailors, appeared in the area. Several of the local products, especially the textiles, soon secured an excellent reputation for the inhabitants of Germantown. The first paper mill in the colonies was established in Germantown by William Rittinghausen (or Rittenhouse) in 1690. Aside from the mill, the Germantowners also built a church, a prison, and a school, where Pastorius held classes.

Germantown grew rapidly and soon incorporated smaller neighboring communities (Crefeld, Krisheim, Sommerhausen), all located along the same road. In Germantown, which was closest to Philadelphia, the road was sixty-five feet wide and lined with peach trees. The modest but comfortable dwellings each stood on three acres of land devoted to trees, flowers, and vegetables. A cross street

forty feet wide led to the marketplace, a thriving community of tradesmen, farmers, and gardeners. Pastorius admired the activity around him and deplored the vanity of
book learning, remarking, "[N]ever have metaphysics and
Aristotelian logic made of a savage a Christian, far less
earned a loaf of bread."

Six years after its founding, on August 12, 1689, Germantown was incorporated as a town, and Pastorius had
the honor of being the first mayor, an office he held four
different times. It was an extremely peaceful and law-abid-
ing community. Crime was practically nonexistent. The
court sat every six weeks but frequently adjourned because
there was no business. Occasionally, a fine was levied for
neglect of fences or a rare case of drunkenness. Two amus-
ing incidents were recorded: A certain Müller was locked
up because of trying to smoke a hundred pipes of tobacco
in one day as a result of a wager; and Caspar Karsten was
incarcerated for calling a policeman a rogue.

Beer was being brewed in the early days of Germantown. Peter Keurlis was in all probability the first beer
brewer in America; he was recorded as having been
granted the privilege of selling beer at a local fair, and in
1695 was summoned before the court because he had run
a saloon on an innkeeper's license.

In 1693 Pastorius and Peter Schuhmacher were com-
missioned to procure stocks for the public punishment of
offenders, yet very little use seems to have been made of
them. In 1697 Arndt Klincken gave his old house for use
as a prison; however, in the same year it was noted in the
Germantown minutes that "all crimes that have been committed previous to this date are to be forgiven, but whatever evil happens henceforward shall not be forgiven."

Pastorius complained in 1703 of the difficulty of finding Germantowners to run for public office. Indeed, to
some holding office was considered a burden, but others

objected on religious grounds. A Mennonite could be excused from public office, but others who refused to participate were fined three pounds for refusal to accept the results of an election. For example, in 1702 Arnold Küster, the ancestor of General George Armstrong Custer, was elected committeeman of Germantown but refused to serve because of conscientious objection. His Mennonite principles, which included not taking an oath, were probably the cause of his refusal. Pastorius expressed the hope that the arrival of new immigrants would alleviate the situation, which apparently it did by the early 1700s.

Pastorius himself set an excellent example in his unselfish and untiring devotion to the community. In fact, the progress and prosperity of the first German settlement in America was largely due to his leadership. He served as burgomaster, town clerk, notary, and member of the Provincial Council. He despised personal gain and asked only for small fees. He was the head of the Quaker School in Philadelphia from 1698 to 1700, and in 1702 he took charge of the school in Germantown, which included a night school for adults.

This must have been highly gratifying to Pastorius, for he was primarily a scholar. In his youth he had studied at the Universities of Altdorf, Strassburg, Basel, and Jena. His learning was clearly encyclopedic, and he had mastered a number of languages. His *Bee Hive* is a neatly written collection of historical, literary, geographical, and poetical works in English, Latin, German, French, Dutch, and Italian. Pastorius published several works dealing with life in the New World, which were influential in encouraging others to immigrate. . . .

Pastorius is also well known for the 1688 poem directed to future generations of German-Americans. This poem, "Hail to Posterity," was widely reprinted and distributed during the 1983 German-American Tricentennial:

Hail to posterity!
Hail, future men of Germanopolis!
Let the young generations yet to be
Look kindly upon this.
Think how your fathers left their native land,—
Dear German-land! O sacred hearths and homes!—
And, where the wild beast roams,
In patience planned
New forest-homes beyond the mighty sea,
There undisturbed and free
To live as brothers of one family
What pains and cares befell,
What trials and what fears,
Remember, and wherein we have done well
Follow our footsteps, men of coming years!
Where we have failed to do
Aright, or wisely live,
Be warned by us, the better way pursue,
And, knowing we were human, even as you,
Pity us and forgive!
Farewell, Posterity!
Farewell, dear Germany!
Forevermore farewell!

Germantown was not only a German-American settlement, but was also the major destination and distribution
center for the colonial German immigration. It also became
the major German-American social, cultural, and political
center. In 1793, President [George] Washington attended a
German service in the Reformed Church there when the
epidemic of yellow fever caused him to move from Philadelphia to Germantown, which was an indication of the
high regard he had for German-Americans. Germantown
itself long remained a cultural center, where books, newspapers, and other publications were printed in German.
The industrial activities and the semiannual fairs provided
exemplary models that were soon adopted elsewhere.

Religious Divisiveness Among Early German Immigrants

Reinhard R. Doerries

Many early German immigrants came to America to escape religious persecution in Germany. However, they brought their religious prejudices with them to their new home. In the following selection Reinhard R. Doerries analyzes how German immigrants splintered into many different religious groups—including Lutherans, Catholics, and Freethinkers—and often feuded among themselves over religious differences. Doerries also describes how the various sects established parochial schools at which immigrant children could learn German and obtain religious instruction. Doerries has been a professor of modern history at several universities in Germany, including the University of Hamburg. He is the author of several books about relations between Germany and the United States, including *Imperial Challenge: Ambassador Count Bernstorff and German-American Relations, 1908–1917.*

The linkage of immigration and religion would appear to be an almost natural consequence of the meaning of faith and worship for most men and women. The linkage was reinforced when people who refused to adopt religious procedures and rituals as prescribed by a ruler, a government, or merely an intolerant society were subjected to persecu-

Reinhard R. Doerries, "Immigrants and the Church: German Americans in Comparative Perspective," *German American Immigration and Ethnicity in Comparative Perspective*, edited by Wolfgang Helbich and Walter D. Kamphoefner. Madison, WI: Max Kade Institute for German-American Studies, 2004. Copyright © 2004 by the Max Kade Institute for German-American Studies. Reproduced by permission.

tion. Bitter wars were fought in the name of religion and over religious issues, and it is not astonishing that immigrants from most countries brought hatred and prejudice, along with their faith, with them to America. Many of the new Americans even exerted great energy trying to rebuild European structures, in the German case, to the point of trying to organize a German state in North America. . . .

No Religious Freedom in Germany

Religious freedom, in the American sense, had not existed in most regions of Europe, and Germany was no exception. Emigration as an act of self-liberation, that is, breaking with one's own past, might, therefore, also be seen as self-liberation from religious intolerance—that suffered from others and that righteously inflicted by oneself on others. While this was true for many immigrants, even those who, if asked, would have given economic reasons for their migration, it is even more true for those who were actually driven from their homeland by the religious bigotry and violence of their compatriots.

German society, torn asunder by the painful religious and social conflicts connected with the Reformation, may serve as an example of a people beset almost continuously by fierce campaigns of religious intolerance and persecution. The forced union of the Lutherans and the Reformed Church, an unrelenting aggressiveness of the Freethinkers toward organized churches, the ostracizing of all so-called sects by both Lutherans and Catholics, and the *Kulturkampf*, the German chancellor's war against the Catholic Church, all illustrate the religious divisiveness apparent in German society throughout much of the nineteenth century. In 1907 Adolf Harnack, a leading German theologian of his time, put it in these words: "Everywhere one meets the colossal prejudice; everywhere one meets the fences, yes, the walls of denominations."

The study of German immigrants to the United States, and, even more so, of their acculturation in American society, would therefore seem to be a futile exercise if faith and religious practice were ignored—as indeed it has been in much of immigration history, not to mention German emigration history. The European churches, with all their inherent structural and doctrinal problems, consciously or unconsciously were brought to America by the immigrants. There, these European churches were confronted by a wide variety of tolerated religious practices, as well as by an older American tradition of the imagination of "religious homogeneity." In that confrontation most European religious institutions, even those brought across the Atlantic by the initially much feared Irish Catholics, underwent considerable alterations and in time came to be considered American. Surely, German immigrants, like most others and in some cases more than others, came to America to escape their past, but they carried with them a specific German culture and with it specific religious persuasions. Upon arrival at least they often acted as though they were determined to maintain German culture unchanged in America. What differentiated the so-called Germans from the French, the English, or even the Irish, was their apparent lack of cohesion. They were sharply divided by regional origin and culture; by such divergent dialects that English, in some cases, became their lingua franca [common language]; by church membership, and often by what can only be called rigid social or class differences. Because faith—and therefore the church—belongs to the personal realm, it is less exposed to normative outside influences. It is, therefore, less quickly challenged than other cultural traditions, meaning that a vital factor in the social control system is more protected than other cultural factors, such as the law or education. . . .

When studying the acculturation processes of Germans

in American society, one of the more pressing questions then would appear to be how much and what kind of faith and religious behaviorism was transported to America by those who left German society, and how was what they brought with them Americanized.

At first glance it seems true that Germans or Prussians, no less than Americans, saw themselves as a chosen people. Yet, it would appear that chosenness was already present at the birth of America, while, by contrast, the German people oppressed by their kings and regional princelings were still struggling for proof of their chosenness, when in World War I they grasped for more power and instead lost what they had gained since 1870/1871. German immigrants then, it is argued here, not unlike other immigrants from Europe, often left a society harshly divided by religious fact, as well as by prejudice, and entered an American society that, however prejudiced, had never experienced the extent and the continuities of religious intolerance common to most of Western European national history. One may well consider religion, among other things, as a matter of the private sphere, as has been done in the past; but it is also true, in spite of all continued tendencies to privatize faith, that faith and the public organization of the faithful have exerted considerable influence on the development of American society.

Bitterness and Feuds

The divisiveness of German Americans in religious matters has been so strong that it has prevented them from dominating any of the large churches in America. Catholics, Lutherans, and Freethinkers spent much of their strength feuding against each other, and the bitterness with which the groups pursued their differences in public was indeed extraordinary. Intolerance often reigned supreme. There is, therefore, nothing on the German American side that

might be compared to the role Irish Americans played in
the Roman Catholic Church. Even German Lutherans in
America, battling each other over the Augsburg Confession[1]
and language maintenance, would not gather in one church
and instead preferred to join other Europeans in splintered
Lutheran synods. They clearly accepted and benefited from
the almost unlimited religious freedom in American society caused by the separation of church and state, as laid
down in the First Amendment to the Constitution: "Congress shall make no law respecting an establishment of religion, or prohibiting the free exercise thereof." They began to behave, in most instances, as other Americans of
various faiths would: They learned to be free and independent of government influences and, like Americans, they,
who often had no experience in freedom and rebellion,
came to oppose the hierarchies in the church and to operate as trustees of their often largely independent parishes.
Lacking the structures of the Italian American campanile
society and not possessing the rich Irish American memory of the endless struggle against Britain, the common
Protestant enemy, German Americans, in most cases, ad-
justed to their surroundings and eventually became Americans. Exceptions, even such developments as the Missouri
Synod with its almost nationalist language maintenance efforts, or Cahenslyism, the German onslaught toward the
end of the nineteenth century against Americanism within
the then strongly Irish American and confident Roman
Catholic Church, merely demonstrate the comparatively serious lack of religious cohesion among the Germans. The
point should not be overstressed, but, in contrast to the
Irish-American takeover of the Roman Catholic Church
from the French, both Wilhelm Löhe's[2] efforts on behalf of
German-American Lutherans and the Catholic Cahenslyite

1. a treatise upon which orthodox Lutheran churches base their teachings   2. German
pastor who financed Lutheran missionaries in America

movement did not come from within American society, but rather received their main impetus from European forces outside of America, pursuing European cultural, as well as religious goals. Carl Schneider in his grand study of *The German Church on the American Frontier* put it straightforwardly: "The general feeling prevailed that the factors of race, folk, and nation were normative for the vital, spiritual development of the Germans in America.". . .

Many Early German Immigrants Were Catholic

Most earlier German immigrants were religious, and it has been said that "their history is therefore largely the history of their churches." Many of them were Lutheran and German Reformed, but the more peripheral German post-Reformation churches, in German society soon outcast as sects, were also represented in North America from the beginning. Moreover, American churches, such as the Methodists, Congregationalists, and Baptists, had made considerable inroads among German immigrants rather early in the nineteenth century, even though these churches were hardly known in Germany then. In several cases, early followers of such churches had migrated from Germany to America only to return to Germany for missionary work several years later. Some of the Germans who were won over by these missionaries later emigrated to America. That Catholics were among the earliest German immigrants, and that they made up a considerable percentage of the Germans coming to America in the hundred years between the Napoleonic Wars and World War I had been largely ignored by historians, even in the United States. Only the influential publications of scholars such as Philip Gleason, Robert Cross, and Colman Barry finally demonstrated that Germans in America often were Catholics. . . .

However personalized faith may be, we can be certain

that institutions and associations of the church played a considerable part in the daily life of the immigrant, thus giving the church also a public quality. For the immigrant, Catholic as well as Lutheran, the institutionalized church was probably one of the most important vehicles in the difficult process of acculturation, the transcending from the familiar and clearly outlined European cultural surroundings to the world of seemingly unlimited choice and opportunity in America. In this respect, immigrants from German regions did not differ from the Scandinavians, the English, the Irish, or later arriving Italians and East Europeans. Protestant or Catholic, in large numbers they turned to the already existing churches of their faith and ritual, and where such did not yet exist, as was often the case, they erected their own, rather than joining one similar to their own. Though often without financial means, they made considerable personal sacrifices to establish parishes using their accustomed ritual and language. Once a group of people had created what might be called a parish, they would obtain a pastor or a priest, and, since in most cases he would have been trained by a particular denomination, he would use his connections and write for help, often from as far away as the country from which he and the immigrants had come.

Crying for help, these letters were written by the hundreds, and they led to the formation of groups having for their main purpose what they saw as mission work among the immigrant churches but what, in fact, often was no more than what we would refer to as a fund drive. . . .

The same kind of Catholic unity stemming from a worldwide Catholic Church was clearly evident in American society where the associationalism of the parishes could freely grow, ignored by the state and protected by a diocesan shield. To be sure, German Lutheran associations also grew in the unencumbered American environment, but they lacked the strength gained from a strong mother church and, it needs to be said, they were not forced to unite as Catholics were, or as Catholics may have thought they were, in view of vociferous and at times aggressive nativist anti-Catholic campaigns. Philip Schaff, a leading German-American Reformed theologian, co-founder of the Evangelical Alliance, and a vociferous supporter of church unity, put it bluntly: "The Lutheran Church in America really is a unit in name only; in fact, it consists of a great number of synods that are quite independent of each other and some of which belong to a quite opposite dogmatic direction."

When immigrant churches finally reached a certain financial security, they did not break off the old ties to forge ahead on their own. To the contrary, the former ties were often reinforced by American money, now flowing back, for instance, to help finance Lutheran seminaries in Germany training pastors for North America. The Evangelical-Lutheran Seminary Eben-Ezer in Kropp and a similar seminary in Breklum are examples of institutions working with funds coming back from the United States. Most of the initiatives, Catholic or Lutheran, and later in America also German Jewish, came from leading individuals, but the financial base was often created by the modest donations from a great number of very average parishioners on both sides of the Atlantic. . . .

Religious Schools Helped Preserve Traditions

Besides the ethnic associations with their often curious amalgamation of religious and socioeconomic purposes, the most significant ethnic activity was directed toward educating the next generation. Schools, however, were for the immigrant not only an economic burden that required a considerable amount of cooperation across class lines, but they were also a prime vehicle for the passage of cultural tradi-

tions to the children. It is true that for the early immigrants, such as the Germans and the Irish, schools were
needed to educate the young, not necessarily to perpetuate
German Lutheran or Catholic or Irish Catholic culture. By
allowing the priests to teach, the church often became the
first institution capable of providing an education.

Later, in the American city, the ethnic school quickly
took on other meanings, one of them, as [authors] Joshua
A. Fishman and Vladimir C. Nahirny put it, being a
counter force against "urban industrial American mass
culture." Since the merits of parochial schools continue to
be a lively issue even in our time, it should be pointed out
that church education organized by newcomers was in existence well before what we call public school systems came
into being. Moreover, the forerunners of today's parochial
schools were not limited to Catholic schools but were also
organized by Lutherans, Quakers, Congregationalists, and
other denominations. In the United States demand for private church-run education has always been high, and the
growth figures from Chicago, showing an increase from 14
schools with 5,770 students in 1865 to 134 schools with
84,429 students in 1910, are not exceptional.

The Catholic Church in America needed some time until a Catholic school system became an official reality in
1884 at the Third Plenary Council in Baltimore. Then,
however, the hierarchy left no doubt as to the seriousness
of its intent: "No parish is complete till it has schools ad-
equate to the needs of its children, and the pastor and
people of such a parish should feel that they have not accomplished their entire duty until the want is supplied."
Evidently, the parishes followed the directive, and the
Catholic school system, as a result, experienced a very im-
pressive growth. Interestingly, while language maintenance
played a major role in the bitter confrontation of Cahenslyism with Americanism, the church school as an institution

or the appointment of, for instance, German- or Polish-speaking priests and nuns in such schools were not among the major issues. Perhaps Cardinal James Gibbons had it right when in 1907 he said about his Catholics: "With the English language as a constantly enlarging part of their course, they are gradually, almost unconsciously, brought into complete sympathy with American ideals, and readily adapt themselves to American manners and customs. This assimilation is constantly going on in our Catholic schools. . . ." Not surprisingly, such foresight as expressed by the open and forward-looking Cardinal, was not shared by the more conservative leaders of the Missouri Synod. For them, the maintenance of German, closely linked to faith and culture, was an essential function of the church school system. Possibly because their Lutheran parishes often were German only, and because no competitive factors were evident as in the Roman Catholic Church where Irish and German interests were set against each other, they insisted on German. The Missouri Synod, in fact, in several cases even rejected English-speaking parishes.

In the final analysis, though, prejudices expressed by both German Lutherans and Irish Catholics turned out to be very similar; both churches voiced loud accusations against the godless state school. On a more positive side, it should be recalled that, of course, the ethnic schools, such as those of the German Freethinkers, who fought the influence of the churches, and the parochial schools served a much needed function for the children of the immigrants: They offered an education. Perhaps, though it is not possible to elaborate within the limits of this paper, it ought to be added that the immigrant by supporting a church school carried a tax burden heavier than that of his American neighbor who sent his children to the public school system.

CHAPTER 2

The Great Waves: German Immigration During the 1800s

COMING TO AMERICA

Nineteenth-Century German Immigrants Sought Economic Prosperity

Roger Daniels

Before the nineteenth century, many Germans immigrated to America because of religious or political repression. As Roger Daniels explains in the following selection, the waves of immigrants during the 1800s came mainly because of the prospect of economic success in the United States. As industrialization changed life in Germany, many Germans saw emigration as the best way to start over. Daniels, a retired professor of history at the University of Cincinnati, is the author of numerous books about immigration, including *Coming to America: A History of Immigration and Ethnicity in American Life*, from which this selection is excerpted.

Superficially, the immigration of Germans during the peak immigration years seems similar to that of the Irish. Between the 1830s and the 1880s Germans were never less than a quarter of all immigrants. They were nearly a third of all foreign born in 1860, 30.9 percent, and a quarter in 1900, 25.7 percent. Between them, Germans and Irish were almost seven out of ten foreign born in the former year, 69.8 percent, and more than four out of ten in the latter, 41.4 percent. Never again would two ethnic groups so dominate immigration. But that, and the fact that both groups were European, were about the only similarities. Germans spoke a foreign language, represented three broad confessional groups—Protestants, Catholics, and Jews—and had a varied pattern of distribution in the United States, participating significantly in both urban pursuits and agriculture. Germans more consistently migrated in family groups and had a return migration rate more than half again as high as that of the Irish, 13.7 percent as against 8.9 percent. Germans were drawn to the United States largely by economic reasons, but they were not fleeing from a national disaster or from a stagnant economy; they were, rather, often persons dislocated or threatened by a vigorous, if uneven, economic growth. Germans and Irish both had ethnic pride, but while Irish Americans could have little identification with the government of Ireland, that "most distressful nation," most German Americans took particular pride in Germany's achievements, especially after the creation of the German Empire, the Second Reich, in 1871. [Author] Mack Walker's observation about nineteenth-century German immigrants, that they came not to establish something new but to reestablish something old, could never be made about the Irish. The cultural apparatus created in the United States by Germans in the nineteenth and early twentieth centuries dwarfs that of any other ethnic group. . . .

America Attracted the Most German Immigrants

There are special problems in trying to decide who is German. Prior to 1871, there was no German nation, but only a collection of separate German states, which in 1871 became unified under Prussian leadership. The chart [accompanying this selection] follows the American data which generally treat as German all persons immigrating from the post-1871 boundaries of Germany. This means that German speakers from Switzerland, Austria, and the Austro-Hungarian Empire, and so on, are not included. My maternal grandmother, for example, a German-speaking Jew from Hungary who arrived in 1900, was almost certainly listed as a Hungarian although she read a German-language newspaper for the rest of her life. In that sense the data understate Germans and Germanness. On the other hand, some German states had ethnic minorities—Poles in Prussia, Danes in Schleswig-Holstein for example—who, if they came to the United States, were almost certain to be counted as Germans. This tends to overstate German immigration. Which factor is more significant no one can say. This counting by nationality rather than ethnicity continues to create problems in American immigration data. Many recent refugees and immigrants from Vietnam and other parts of Southeast Asia are ethnic Chinese who so identify themselves to the census taker, but who are recorded in the immigration

Immigrants from Germany, 1820–1924

DECADE	NUMBER	PERCENTAGE OF TOTAL IMMIGRATION
1820–30	7,729	5.1
1831–40	152,454	25.4
1841–50	434,626	25.3
1851–60	951,667	36.6
1861–70	787,468	34.0
1871–80	718,182	25.5
1881–90	1,452,970	27.7
1891–1900	505,152	13.7
1901–10	341,498	3.9
1911–20	143,945	2.5
1921–24	148,102	6.3
Total	5,643,793	

data as citizens of the nation of their birth.

Although some German immigrants headed to Russia and other less-developed parts of central and eastern Europe (large numbers of their descendants would eventually come to the United States) and others migrated to such destinations as Argentina, Brazil, Canada, and South Africa, once the postcolonial migration of Germans to America had got under way in the mid-1830s, about 90 percent of all German immigrants came to the United States. The rhythms of their movements were largely affected by the fluctuations of the American business cycle, although, to be sure, economic and political events within Germany also had their effect.

Religion and Politics Were Not Motivating Factors

Religious motivations, so important in establishing the colonial American migrations, were much less significant in the nineteenth century. Some Old Lutherans from Prussia were impelled to come by the unification of their church with the Reformed Church in the 1830s, and small handfuls of religious radicals, mostly pietists, founded new societies in Pennsylvania and, as the century progressed, in Ohio, Iowa, South Dakota, and the prairie provinces of Canada, chiefly Alberta. Among Catholics, [German chancellor Otto von] Bismarck's *Kulturkampf* (cultural struggle) against them shortly after unification was a push factor.

Politics was even less significant as a pushing force. The Metternichian [suppressive] reaction after the defeat of Napoleon and the sometimes violent repression of liberalism in the 1830s did send some activists abroad. Even the great upheavals following the failed revolutions of 1848 made a very small numerical contribution to total emigration, and the legend of the forty-eighters [refugees from the revolution] in the German American community has been greatly inflated. It is true that some exiles did flee to the United States after 1848 (many also went to London, including the most famous exile of them all, Karl Marx, but at most there were a few thousand of them). One or two—most notably Carl Schurz (1829–1906), who became a general in the Union Army, represented Missouri in the Senate, and served as Rutherford B. Hayes's secretary of the interior—did have significant American political careers. But as opposed to the Irish, not many Germans were attracted by American politics. Despite all the ink that has been spilled about the failure of an Irish Catholic to be elected president until 1960, it is almost never remarked that no member or descendant of the larger German American community was elected until 1952, and Dwight Eisenhower was elected largely because he had led the armies that defeated Germany. The Kaiser's ambassador to the United States before and during World War I, Count Johann Heinrich von Bernstorff (1862–1939) tells us in his memoirs that his illusions about the potential political power of the German American community were shattered when he visited Milwaukee, the large city with the highest proportion of Germans, and found that it had an *irisch Bürgermeister* ("Irish mayor"). In addition it should be noted that a few German Marxists came to the United States, as did, even more notoriously, some German anarchists. After several of their number were hanged—on no real evidence—for the Haymarket bombings in Chicago (1886), the German radical became, for a time, a stock figure in American social novels, most notably William Dean Howells's *A Hazard of New Fortunes* (1890). The surviving anarchists were eventually pardoned by another German immigrant prominent in American politics, Illinois governor John Peter Altgeld (1847–1902), who was also a very successful businessman.

It was in the economic sphere that the motivations for

most German immigrants were to be found. It was the economics of prosperity, not of poverty, that impelled most of them. What students of socioeconomic change now call "modernization"—industrialization, urbanization, and the whole complex of political and social changes usually attendant with them—was nowhere on the Continent more apparent than in Germany from the mid-nineteenth century onward. These changes in the traditional structure of society made it increasingly difficult to maintain former ways of life. When population growth had been slow or nonexistent it was often possible for sons to succeed fathers, whether in ownership of land or in skilled trade. Increasingly, this became difficult under the new conditions, and, faced with the necessity of moving to a new job, many Germans found emigration a rational alternative. Others, having initially made an internal move—say from a German farm or village to a German city—would then make a further move overseas.

A German Immigrant Decries Anti-Immigrant Violence

Christian Lenz

Election riots resulting from the efforts of the anti-immigrant "Know-Nothings" to curtail the voting rights of immigrants inspired Christian Lenz, a German immigrant living in Louisville, Kentucky, to write a letter to his brother in Germany. In it he described the horrors he had witnessed as well as his fear and disappointment about his new life in America. He warns his brother to stay in Germany—the hardships there were better than the violence in America, despite the potential for prosperity, he argued.

Luisville, October 22nd, 1855

Dear brother, since I have waited so long for your letter but I don't hear or see one so I will write again. . . . You write about the children if I want to have them come or not, I already wrote you in the last letter that the Germans are unwanted in America, but from last February till now it's cost a lot of blood, on August 6th there was an election in Louisville where they had it in for the Germans and those from Aierland [Ireland], they wanted to cast their votes like always but they got beaten and pushed around, then there was a real fight with much bloodshed, the Americans

Christian Lenz, "Farmers," *News from the Land of Freedom: German Immigrants Write Home*, edited by Walter D. Kamphoefner, Wolfgang Helbich, and Ulrike Sommer, translated by Susan Carter Vogel. Ithaca, NY: Cornell University Press, 1991. Copyright © 1988 by C.H. Beck'sche Verlagsbuchhandlung. English translation copyright © 1991 by Cornell University. Reproduced by permission of the publisher.

got shot at from all the houses where many were staying inside, they got fed up with this and set fire to the houses,
destroyed many dwellings, murdering, burning and robbing what they could get, they hanged, burned, cut off
people's heads, shot. In short many people lost their lives
in these days, Germans and Americans, many women and
children that they wouldn't let out of the houses burned
to death. Dear brother I watched how they ran through the
streets like the screaming seven[1] to see human blood. Since
that time many Germans have fled and have moved away,
one this way and the other that way. Now dear brother
should anyone else move to America, no—stay where you
were born that is your home, if I were still in Germany I
wouldn't look at America, even if there's nothing besides
bread and potatoes and salt that is still better than meat
three times a day in a foreign country. . . . The cooper
trade is good, many other *Proffionen* [professions] are at
a standstill. I didn't earn much this summer because I was
sick all the time, I have made a lot of money in the last
weeks when I could work the whole week I earned 22
guilders, but now the last 3 weeks I haven't earned anything, I had fever again, we have a mutual aid society in our
church which I am in too, a sick man gets 7½ guilders a
week that's a great thing, every craftsman pays 38 kreuzers
a month. . . .

Your true brother,
Christian Lenz

1. This is a possible reference to the Apocalypse, in which the imminent end of the
world is depicted in the form of symbolic images and visions. Here, in connection with
disasters and afflictions, the number seven plays a central role.

A Civil War Letter

Carl Schurz

As a group, German Americans were generally opposed to slavery and to the concept of secession by the southern states. As a result of these beliefs and because military service offered a good livelihood, the Union Army was composed of a high proportion of German immigrants. One such German American was Carl Schurz, a lawyer from Milwaukee, Wisconsin, who was appointed brigadier general of volunteers in the Union Army. In the following letter from Schurz, written during the war to his ten-year-old daughter, Agathe, he explains why he is committed to the Union cause. After the war Schurz served in the U.S. Senate and was secretary of the interior under President Rutherford B. Hayes.

To His Daughter Agathe, Camp in Lookout Valley, Tennessee, November 9, 1863

This evening it is so delightfully warm and pleasant in my tent; my fire burns brightly, and out yonder in the camp I hear the retiring signal. Now I will answer your dear letter.

I am very glad indeed that you wrote to me, and the news which you give is exceedingly agreeable. It is nice that you are once more going to school, and if you will be industrious I do not doubt that you will soon overtake the big girls in your acquirement. I have an idea that you are somewhat behind in your arithmetic, and you should apply yourself particularly in that subject. Arithmetic must

Carl Schurz, "Intimate Letters of Carl Schurz, 1841–1869," *Pioneering the Upper Midwest: Books from Michigan, Minnesota, and Wisconsin, ca. 1820–1910*, edited and translated by Joseph Schafer. Madison: State Historical Society of Wisconsin, 1928.

be practiced, and when you have made some progress therein you will pursue it with genuine pleasure. Geography will be particularly easy for you. You have already seen many more strange lands than most children of your age and you will be able to find on the map many widely separated places in which you have already been. You always enjoyed world history, and that pleases me greatly. It is the most educative and the pleasantest of all studies. I desire also that you pursue your piano playing industriously and that you learn to draw. That is an activity which is equally pleasant and useful, and a source of satisfaction throughout life. You have observed how much pleasure Mama and I get out of music, and I have often regretted that I did not learn drawing properly. But now my youth is past. I am almost too old to learn new things, and besides I have too many other things to do.

I am sure, dear Hans,[1] that you will do everything to give your mother and me pleasure and cause to be satisfied with you. We love you with all our hearts, and you of course love your parents in the same way. It is a great happiness to have good children, and this happiness you will surely bestow upon us. Your good mother suffers a great deal on account of my absence, and you must make it as easy as possible for her to bear her loneliness and her anxiety about me. Perhaps you do not yet understand how much you can help towards that end.

War Is a Holy Cause

I am engaged in a war for a very great and holy cause, whose decision will have tremendous results for the future of the human race. For that reason I am bringing to it great sacrifice and often endure want and weariness and danger. In all of this, the consciousness of having in you a

---

1. most likely an affectionate nickname

good child is a very great consolation. I think of you often, every day, with much love and much confidence, and I know you do everything to make me proud of you.

You must not think however, my good Hans, that things are going badly with us here. My little tent is a genuine picture of comfort; it is as warm here as in a stone house. Also, I have received a present of a feather bed, so that I sleep as soft as a prince. We have plenty of provisions, and though there is no great variety of food there is also no deficiency. It is sometimes a good thing to be obliged to give up things which one generally considers necessary, for that gives us a satisfaction which is a source of content for life.

Actually, we soldiers live much better than the natives of the country. You have no conception of the poverty which prevails here. The people live in log houses in which the chinks between the logs are entirely open so that light and air pass through. Naturally our tents are much tighter and better. Women and men are dressed in the most poverty-stricken way and live almost exclusively on corn bread and pork. Nearly all females smoke and chew tobacco. And then they are so ignorant that the knowledge of reading and writing is a great rarity among them. The difference between this population and that which we see in the North is tremendous. But there is a quite natural cause for it. In this country, the state of Tennessee, which you can easily find on the map, slavery prevails. There are here a few rich people who own many negroes. These negroes do all the work for them and the rich gentlemen therefore gain the idea that they themselves were not born to work but rather to govern and rule. They did not want to rule merely their negroes but also, particularly, the poor white people who did not have enough money to buy slaves and for that reason were forced to work themselves. In order to rule them better the rich people sought to keep the poor ignorant, and so it came about that there are very few schools here and most people have enjoyed no instruction whatever. Since they know nothing of the many discoveries and appliances which have been made during the past century they remain poor and miserable.

Hope for the Future

For these people and their children the present war is a genuine blessing, for it shakes them out of their sleepiness and brings them in touch with keener and more active people. They become aware how miserable their condition is; their indolent habits are interfered with; they are compelled to help themselves and are thereby forced to turn their thoughts toward new things. They hear how very different life is in other sections of the country, and later, when in the train of this war other people come to settle here, they will be influenced by the industry around them; for the country itself is beautiful and fruitful, and an industrious people could live happily and amass much wealth. That will certainly happen after the war, for the northern men who came down here with the army already see what beautiful regions there are in the South and what splendid opportunities can be found here for human activity. So you see how good can come out of evil. The war is certainly in itself a very great misfortune and brings frightful distress to large numbers. But some of its results will be highly beneficial to mankind.

Now, my dear Agathe, I must say adieu for today. Love me much; be good to our little Pussy [Schurz's daughter Marianna], who, as you know, has not yet attained the age of discretion and must be gently dealt with; be dutiful toward Mama; and write me soon again. You will give me great joy thereby.

German American Life and Culture in Nineteenth-Century Texas

Lucinda Permien Holze

For the Germans who chose Texas as the place to start their new lives in America, an adventurous spirit was necessary. The following interview with Lucinda Permien Holze, who came to Texas in 1873, tells of the challenges she and her family faced. She also shares the stories of earlier immigrants to Texas, stories handed down to her by friends and family. These tales reveal how important it was for German Americans to band together, both to succeed in their new country and to preserve the culture and customs they brought with them from Germany. This interview is from the Works Progress Administration American Life Histories Collection of 1936–1940.

I was born in the year 1857 in Mechlenburg, Germany. My father, Ludwig Permien, emigrated to America in the year 1871. He settled at the town of Fredericksburg, Texas. When he was located he sent for my folks in the year 1873. By this time he had become a naturalized American citizen. The war between the states was over and the worst of the reconstruction days were past. But there were still some Indians in the western part of the state where we came.

Lucinda Permien Holze, "Interview with Mrs. Lucinda Permien Holze," transcribed by Effie Cowan. Library of Congress, WPA Federal Writers' Project Collection, 1936–1940.

The country was mostly a stock and ranch country, but in between the hills there was timber and so they raised their grain in these valleys. When they took their stock and produce to the markets they went to San Antonio, Austin and Brownsville. There were lots of Mexicans near our town and the German settlers employed them to clear the brush from the land they put in cultivation and to help herd the cattle. There were a very few slaves at this time in Gillespie County. The settlers lived in log cabins and the schools and churchs also were the log houses.

The schools were the one-teacher schools and the teachers would board around with the families of their pupils, and the salaries were around twenty-five dollars a month. After I was grown I went to Austin and helped do housework for the white women. Then in 1879 I married Mr Frederick Holze and moved near the town of Brenham, Texas, to a little village named Industry.

Texas Towns Were Dangerous

For many years my husband operated a little country store at this place. I have heard him tell about when he was a sixteen year old boy during the Civil War, how he was a teamster and drove the freight wagons from Industry to Brenham and on down to the nearest railroad. The wagon trains would go together to protect each other from the robbers. Sometimes when they were passing thro' the river bottom the robbers would take their wagon's with the freight and the team's the men would be [glad] to escape with their lives.

I can remember when I lived in Austin how the rangers would be stationed over on the Concho river to watch for the Indians. They were still giving trouble, robbing the settlers of their stock and their grain. I can also remember the old court house in Austin. It was located down near the Colorado river. The course of the river ran thro' the city making a very picturesque picture with its large trees that bordered the banks of the river.

When the river was on a rise we crossed on the ferry boats and when it was low it was easy to ford it as the bed of the river was rock. Sometimes in the spring it would get on a big rise and overflow the lowlands near the city. The people who lived in these places would have to move to higher ground. It was about the time I left Austin in 1879 that they built the new capitol.

After I came to Industry, near Brenham, I was surprised to see such large farms, they called them plantations, they were situated close to the river's, the Brazos and Little River, and many were called the Bottom plantations. The soil was very rich and they often made a bale of cotton to the acre. There were so many more negroes. They had been slaves of the plantation owners and since their freedom they were working the land for their former owners and the owners giving them part of the crops for their work.

The towns of Brenham and Industry are near Little River, as well as the Brazos, and sometimes it overflowed too, and the Santa Fe rail-road would be under water and the trains delayed for days at a time. The white people lived away from the bottom but the negro cabins were down on these plantations and it was common for the white people to have to go and bring them out in boats when the overflow's occurred.

The German Settlement of Perry

In 1884 my husband brought his family to the German settlement near what is now Perry, Texas. We owned a little store and he was postmaster at a little place called Stamps. It was at this place that we had our experience with robbers. One afternoon as we were ready to close the store, two men rode up on horse-back, came in and asked for tobacco. As my husband turned to get it, they drew a gun on him and told him to give them all the money he had.

At the same time the other one turned to me and told me that if I made a noise that he would shoot me, then he turned to help the man who held the gun on my husband rob the cash drawer and safe. When he did this I ran to a neighbor's and gave the alarm, but when the neighbor got there they had the money and were gone. We never did recover of our money or find the robbers.

I will not attempt to give you the story of the German settlement at Perry, but there was a young man from Germany by the name of Von Holwegg who was among the colony that Mr Schlimbech brought over. This young Holwegg accumalated [sic] a large amount of property and made Mr Otto Rau his overseer. Mr Rau also was one of the first ones to come over from Germany with this colony. My son Louis married his daughter and after Mr Rau died, he took charge of this property and is the agent yet.

I have five living children, they are Mrs L.H. Schmidt [of] Riesel, with whom I make my home. Mr Louis Holze [of] Waco. Mr E.J. Holze, Otto, Texas, and a daughter, Mrs A.L. Leifeste of Houston, Texas. My husband passed away in 1918 at the age of sixty-nine years.

History of German Communities

Yes; I can give you a little of the history of the early days of some of the German communities in Texas before the Civil War came, as handed down to the descendents of those who were among the first settlers. It is said that in the spring of 1846 the first train for Fredericksburg, consisting of twenty wagons and some two-wheel Mexican carts, left the town of New Braunfels for the new settlement on the Pedernales [River]. There were about 120 men, women and children in this train, accompanied by eight of the soldiers furnished by the "Society for the Protection of German Immigrants in Texas."

After a trip lasting sixteen days they arrived at the future town of Fredericksburg. It is worthy of note that the meat for the first meal served to them in this new location was bear meat. John Schmidt, one of the military soldiers shot a bear on the banks of the Pedernales river.

The immigrants passed a band of Indians just before they crossed the river and when they heard the shot from the rifle, they thought it was an Indian attack, but it was only the hunters shooting at the bear. Another soldier killed a panther just before they crossed the river. The timber here was dense and the animals were plentiful.

A partial list of the first settlers has been kept, but the full list seems to have been lost since the county clerks records were destroyed by fire in 1850. Among the family names are Ahelger, Schmidt, Lochte, Bonn, Berbens, Schwars, Strackbein, Durst, Syeubing, Heinmann, Llein, Leydendecker, Eckhardt, Neffendorf, Theile, Schneider, Fritz, Weidenfeld, and Schnautz.

First School, First Churches

It is a matter of record that the first school in Fredericksburg was organized by the "Society for the Protection of German Immigrants in Texas." John Leydendecker held the school in the church building. When the first city school was organized in 1856 August Siemering was chosen as the teacher. By 1860 there were ten schools in the settlement around Fredericksburg and an enrollment of 260 pupils. In 1860 the number of white people in the country was around twenty-seven hundred, thirty-three slaves and thirty-eight people in business.

The first religious service for the German immigrants was held in the city of Houston in Dec. 1839 and in a short while there were regular services held for them in the city by a Mr Evendberg who came to Houston from Illinois in 1839. In the year's 1840 to 1844 this Mr Evendberg and Mr Johann Anton Fisher organized Protestant churches in Industry, Cat Springs, Biegel, La Grange and Colombus. The Catholices also had churches in New Braunfels and Fredericksburg. The first mass was celebrated in New Braunfels by a priest named George Menzel, who in the same year built a cross on the Kreuzberg mountain, to the northwest of Fredericksburg to show to the world the Catholic standard as a symbol of salvation and civilization.

The first Methodist church organized in Fredericksburg was in the year 1849 and Rev. Eduard Schneider organised it and held the services in the societies hall until 1855 when the congregation built a church house for themselves.

German American Social Life

On the eve of Whitsuntide[1] the German's of Industry and Cat Springs organized a German order under the leadership of Friederich Ernst, which was to further immigration and correspondence between Germany and Texas and to preserve the German traits. To belong to this order the requisites were talent, ability and education. In March 1843 the members showed their patriotism of Texas by celebrating the [anniversary] of Texas Independence. After this there were organized various clubs and societies for the social life of the communities.

In telling of the social life of the German people of that day my story would not be complete without telling you of the invisible passenger that came with these first families, and that was the talent for music as expressed both with instruments and in song. To the march across the wilderness of this state it accompanied them and helped them to win in their struggles against the hardships of the life of the pioneer.

The first singing society in Texas was organized at New Braunfels in March 1850. It was called the "Germania."

1. seventh Sunday after Easter, commemorating the coming of the Holy Spirit to the Apostles

Some of its first directors were Petmecky, C.F. Blum, Dr Adolf Douai, and H. Guenther. Besides the Germania two other clubs were organized at New Braunfels before 1861, they were a chorus of men and women, one was called the "Concordia". There was a quartette at Sisterdale composed of men and at Comfort there was a quartette composed of Ernst Altgelt, Fritz Goldbeck, C.W. Boerner and Fritz Holekamp under the direction of Hermann Schimmel-pfennig.

In August 1853 there was a state song festival (Staats-Saengerfest) with the above mentioned singing societies taking part together with others from San Antonio and Austin. There were four other state meetings before 1861 at New Braunfels and Fredericksburg but when the Civil War was declared then the song festivals were ended for the duration of the war.

Pioneer Culture

The culture of the pioneer German people was also mani-fested in the art of painting, and what wonderful colors to draw their inspiration from! In the spring the landscape was brilliant with the wild flowers, the blue-bonnet, the In-dian blanket with its coat of red, and the "Yellow Rose of Texas" (the song the confederate soldiers loved so well to march by), as well as many other flowers of equal beauty.

Hermann Lungkwitz was one of the most prominent of the landscape painters. His scene of Bear Mountain near Fredericksburg, the Pedernales River, Marble Falls on the Colorado and Waller Creek at Austin are among his best work.

Two of Lungkwitz's painting's hang on the walls of the south entrance hall of the State Capitol Building. One is that of David Crockett, and the other shows the surrender of Santa Anna to Gen. Sam Houston. The portraits to these painting's were done by the artist [William Henry] Huddle, but the landscapes are the works of Hermann Lungkwitz.

The success of the German settlements in Texas is due to a great extent to the "Society for the Protection of German Immigrants in Texas." The immigrants came to Texas to escape oppression in their country and to enjoy the blessing's of liberty and the rights of citizenship. This they accomplished and at the same time their ways, customs and characteristics were preserved.

Then here's to our state, our own dear state,
Right or wrong, oppressed or free;
In poverty and wealth, enthroned or disowned,
Our mother our queen shall be.
Oh! the Lone Star State our home shall be,
As long as her rivers run into the sea.

Stereotypes of German Americans

Frederick C. Luebke

By the 1890s German immigrants made up approximately 10 percent of the U.S. population. Most Americans had at least some contact with German immigrants, and they naturally formed stereotypes of the newcomers. In this selection Frederick C. Luebke discusses how German Americans were perceived by the population at large and how the immigrants' careful preservation of German culture sometimes led to problems. Although many natives thought the immigrants celebrated too often and drank too much beer, in general, German Americans were held in high esteem, seen as industrious and honest. The author is a retired professor of history at the University of Nebraska, Lincoln. He is the author of many books and articles on German immigrants, including *Immigrants and Politics: The Germans of Nebraska, 1880–1900* and *Germans in the New World: Essays in the History of Immigration*, the source of the following selection.

In the 1890s, following a decade of unprecedented immigration from Europe, the United States experienced a period in which national identity was greatly stressed. The term *Americanization* came into frequent usage as many citizens, privately and through various organizations, stressed conformity to the dominant culture in language, manners, and religious belief. . . .

German immigrants and their children were conspicuous. . . . Approximately five million Germans had arrived in the United States during the nineteenth century. In each of the peak years of 1854 and 1882 more than two hundred thousand persons arrived. Although 85 percent of the Germans settled in the northeastern quarter of the country, they could be found in all states of the Union. Two-thirds lived in urban places (a proportion much higher than that for the American population generally at that time), but they were also strongly attracted to agriculture, especially dairy farming in the Midwest. By the end of the century there were about eight million first- and second-generation Germans in the United States, roughly 10 percent of the total population. Unusually diverse in origin, occupation, residence patterns, and religious belief, they were easily the largest non-English-speaking group in America. . . .

Good and Bad Stereotypes

Stereotypes naturally developed. . . . Society tended to regard the Germans in their midst as a unified group with common characteristics. Provincial differences, linguistic variations, religious divisions, and social and political distinctions were usually lost on the native-born, who tended to lump all German immigrants together on the basis of their presumably common language. Because Germany did not exist as a unified state until 1871, a German was simply someone who spoke the German language.

There was no uniform or consistent content to the images of the German immigrant. Wealthy and educated Americans, for example, generally registered more favorable impressions than did the lower classes. Rarely rubbing shoulders with ordinary newcomers, these Americans more often encountered persons who had adapted quickly to American ways and who, like themselves, were educated and successful. Moreover, their impressions were conditioned by notions about Germany itself, such as the preeminence of German learning. In the nineteenth century, approximately ten thousand Americans had studied in various German universities. They discovered a quality of scholarship, a depth of thought, and an appreciation for learning and academic freedom that led them to place Germany on a cultural pedestal. Although such impressions of Germany and its institutions must be separated from ideas about German immigrants, they contributed to a generally high regard for them among the upper strata of society.

Ordinary Americans of the nineteenth century, however, had little contact with the products of German universities and still less with their books and essays. Instead, impressions of things German were gained from ordinary contacts with German-born barbers, bartenders, cobblers, cooks, and seamstresses, or with immigrants who lived next door or on a nearby farm, worked in the same factory, or deposited savings in the same bank.

Perhaps the most prominent elements in the American stereotype of German immigrants were industriousness, thrift, and honesty—admirable virtues in the American value system. The German male seemed strongly attached to his family; he was orderly, disciplined, and stable. A bit too authoritarian by American standards, he was nonetheless admired for his ability to achieve material success through hard work. Similarly attractive was his reputation for mechanical ingenuity. The Germans were usually perceived as an intelligent people, although somewhat plodding in their mental processes. And if they tended to be unimaginatively thorough, they sometimes also seemed stubborn and graceless in manner. But the German wife and mother was commonly regarded as a model of cleanliness and efficiency; her daughter was valued as a reliable house servant or maid. Although some native Americans thought that the Germans treated their women badly, on the whole they considered these newcomers desirable additions to the American population.

Cultural Clashes

But there were negative elements in the image as well. Some felt that Germans were unwarrantably proud of their origins and culture. Others had ambivalent feelings about German festivities. It seemed as though the Germans had a celebration for every occasion, complete with parades and contests both athletic and cultural. Even their church affairs often took a festive air. Especially offensive was what puritanical Americans perceived as abandoned dancing and boorish swilling of beer, especially on the Sabbath, the day that God had set aside for worship, rest, and spiritual contemplation. Still others were put off by the apparent radicalism of German immigrants. The American labor movement seemed to have among its leaders an unusually large number of Germans who preached alien doctrines of communism, anarchism, and varying degrees of socialism. Impressions drawn from such unfortunate and widely publicized affairs as the Chicago Haymarket Riot of 1886[1] strengthened the image of at least some Germans as dangerous revolutionaries.

Clashes between native and immigrant cultures produced some of the most potent political issues of the late nineteenth century. Although many German immigrants were interested in political reform, economic development, and the tariff and currency questions, they responded more strongly to issues related to ethnocultural conflict. In addition to political and economic liberties, they wanted social and cultural freedom. By the 1890s prohibition had become the dominant political manifestation of cultural conflict. Women's suffrage, Sabbatarianism, and efforts to

1. a labor riot in which several German American men were accused and convicted (despite a lack of evidence) of throwing a bomb that killed twelve people

regulate (if not close down) parochial school education were closely related issues that were capable of producing remarkable, although temporary, levels of uniformity in the voting behavior of German immigrants.

Ethnocultural politics had an impact on nativist attitudes.[2] Awareness of ethnic group identities was greatly intensified among immigrants and nativists alike. Thinking in stereotypes and symbols was encouraged; tolerance and understanding diminished. The live-and-let-live attitudes common in earlier decades were weakened by organized political action. Changes in attitudes toward immigrants were also fostered by some of the most respected social scientists of the day, whose study of the immigration question led them to conclude that socially undesirable characteristics were hereditary and were more typical of some ethnic groups than of others. Both negative and positive qualities were thus thought to be fixed or rigid.

German Americans Fared Well

Still, as such ideas gained currency at the end of the nineteenth century, the German Americans fared well. Although there were dissents from the general view, most Americans considered the Germans to be a desirable people. Moreover, as racial thinking became increasingly common early in the twentieth century, some German-American intellectuals were stimulated, in countless speeches and articles, to laud and magnify the achievements of their group, ranging from such early contributions as those of Baron von Steuben in the Revolutionary War to the more recent accomplishments of such engineers as John Roebling and his American-born son, who designed and built the Brooklyn Bridge. This indulgence in cultural chauvinism was partly an effort to lay claim to

2. Nativism favored the interests of established residents over those of immigrants.

a share in American greatness, but it was also intended to balance Anglo-Saxonist notions of racial superiority and preeminence in world affairs.

By the beginning of World War I, the leaders of the rapidly assimilating German element in the United States, understandably proud of their cultural heritage, were encouraged in their ethnocentrism by the stereotypes native-born Americans generally held of them. Some were even prompted to promote their heritage as a culture counter to the dominant Anglo-American. But this was a dangerous course in a period of resurgent nativism. Deviations from American norms were but lightly tolerated by persons unwilling or unable to distinguish cultural chauvinism from the political or nationalistic variety.

The Rise of the German American Beer Barons

Carl H. Miller

Immigrants brought their love of beer with them from Germany, and many were able to establish a livelihood based solely on its production and sale. In fact, most of the major breweries in America were established by German immigrants. In the following selection Carl H. Miller details the rise of the "beer barons," German immigrants who established these breweries. He also explains how beer served as a catalyst for social interaction among the immigrant community, and he describes the lively beer gardens that served as a social venue. This "golden age" of beer-making ended, however, with the Prohibition movement, which resulted in a complete alcohol ban from 1920 to 1933. Miller, an expert on the history of beer, is the author of *Breweries of Cleveland*.

Captain Frederick Pabst strode proudly through the various departments of his Milwaukee brewery. Flanked by a guest, New York Governor Roswell P. Flowers, the Captain was always at his best when showing off his world-class brewery to some visiting dignitary. The Governor could not help but to be impressed by the sheer enormity of the Pabst operation—the gargantuan copper brew kettles stretching two stories in height, the towering oak fermenters capped by pillows of white foam, the endless rows of rotund casks filled with aging beer, and the army of

Carl H. Miller, "The Rise of the Beer Barons," *All About Beer*. Reproduced by permission.

busy German workers tending to their various duties. The Captain was particularly proud of the brewery's work force. Many years spent as a steamship captain on Lake Michigan taught him the value of employing only the strongest and fittest men. Wishing to boast this to his guest, Pabst could not resist an impromptu demonstration.

"You see that fire bucket hanging on the wall?" asked Captain Pabst. "Any of my men can fill that pail with beer and drink it down as you would a glassful." Turning to a nearby employee to prove it, the Captain said in a raised voice, "Isn't that so, Pete?"

"Ja, Herr Captain," replied the worker, "but would you excuse me just one minute?"

The worker retreated to an adjacent room. Upon his return, he filled the fire bucket with beer, hoisted it to his mouth, and proceeded to drain it in one long pull. Amazed and impressed by the feat, the Governor and the Captain congratulated the beaming employee and proceeded with their tour of the brewery. A curious Captain Pabst later asked the worker why it had been necessary to leave the room before emptying the bucket. The employee replied, somewhat embarrassed, "Vell, Captain, I didn't know for sure could I do it. So I just went to try it first."

Models of Success

Indeed, life inside a 19th-century American brewery required, at minimum, a hearty disposition. The work was arduous and the hours long. But, for many German immigrants, working in a brewery was a coveted privilege. Particularly within German-American enclaves, the local brewery was often the nucleus of its neighborhood. Lager beer, after all, was at the heart of daily life for many German immigrants, and its makers took great pride in producing the best they could. Brewmasters commanded unmatched respect, enjoying the status of virtual nobility. And the brewery owners—with their great wealth and position in the community—embodied the very success of the German people in America.

Their prosperity was made possible by the more than four million Germans who departed their homeland for new life in America throughout the last half of the 19th century. Not surprisingly, the Germans' timeless affinity for beer was one of the few precious traditions not left behind in the great exodus. As droves of immigrants landed on American shores, beermaking entered a new era. Names like Busch, Pabst, Schlitz, Ruppert, Ehret and many others became synonymous with beer, and were soon destined to rank among the greatest names in all of American industry. Without question, the age of the "Beer Barons" had arrived.

The utter transformation of the American beer scene by the Germans, although astonishingly rapid, was not immediate. Most of the men who would come to rule the industry—and amass great wealth doing it—came from typically humble beginnings. One observer painted a rather unflattering picture of the early immigrant brewer:

> The German artisan who founded the American beer industry was a kind of special cook with a trade recipe he had learned in Germany. He began by boiling beer in small quantities in family kettles or wash-boilers, and often, with his wife, retailed it to a German trade in a small saloon. The man and wife were typical Germans of the working class—industrious, frugal, honest, and rather unsophisticated. The old-time brewmaster worked in necessarily uncleanly underground cellars, full of the drip of great ice-houses overhead, and of quantities of carbonic acid gas, sufficient to smother small animals, below; with floors saturated with the organic matter of former brews, and slippery with the molds that grow under such conditions. In this place he tramped—a heavy figure in a slouch hat, coarse workman's clothes, and high

leather boots. But for his special cook's knowledge of brewing, he dominated the brewing industry.

Empires on the Rise

The earliest of the German brewers in America brewed, by necessity, only top-fermented English style brews—mainly ales and stouts. Not until the 1840s and 50s, with the arrival of bottom-fermenting lager beer yeast from Europe, could German brewers produce the Bavarian-style lagers and golden pilsners that would ultimately become their trademark in America. Reflecting on the long-anticipated arrival of lager beer in his town, one old immigrant commented, "To have lager beer from the tap in the land of hard liquor, what German friendly to drinking could not have felt the pull of home?"

And feel it they did. By the mid-1870s, the number of breweries operating in America had blossomed to an astounding 4,000. Over the next twenty-five years, the nation's beer production soared from about 10 million barrels (31 gallons per barrel) to nearly 40 million barrels per year. Brewery owners who once spent 18-hour days slaving over malt kilns and brew kettles now began to reap the rewards of their labor. As the never-ending stream of European immigration continued to flow, beermaking dynasties were being forged in virtually every city in the nation. Almost exclusively, Germans were at the helm.

In St. Louis, Adolphus Busch was busy transforming his father-in-law's (Eberhard Anheuser's) once-failing brewery into a grand empire. Adolphus, perhaps more than any other brewer, became known for his flamboyant, almost audacious persona. Tirelessly promoting his Budweiser beer, he toured the country in a luxurious railroad car immodestly named "The Adolphus." In place of the standard calling card, the young entrepreneur presented friends and business associates with his trademark gold-plated pocket knife featuring a peephole in which could be viewed a likeness of Adolphus himself. His workers bowed in deference as he passed. "See, just like der king!" he liked to say.

In New York City, brewery owner George Ehret enjoyed a similar majesty. Affectionately nicknamed "the crazy Dutchman" despite his German birth, Ehret was the quintessential beer baron. Within a mere dozen years after its founding in 1866, Ehret's Hell Gate Brewery (named for the neighborhood in which it was located) was producing more beer than any other brewery in the country. Investing much of his profit in real estate, the crazy Dutchman ultimately ranked near the infamous Astors in the value of his property holdings in the city.

However, it was one of Ehret's competitors, brewer Jacob Ruppert, who won the hearts of New Yorkers. Colonel Ruppert, as he was known, bought the New York Yankees in 1915 and transformed the struggling baseball team into the American League powerhouse of their day. Using his vast beer profits, the Colonel built Yankee Stadium and bought talent like Babe Ruth and Waite Hoyt. During the twenty-four years the Colonel owned the team, the Yankees won seven World Championships and boasted some of history's greatest players.

Milwaukee: The Brew City

Of course, there were no beer barons like those of Milwaukee—the city virtually built on malt and hops. The unmatched quantities of beer consumed in the brew city during the 19th century gave rise to the popular term "Milwaukee goiter," used to refer to a rounded belly. A well-known joke of the day said that every kitchen sink in Milwaukee had three faucets—one for hot water, one for cold water, and the biggest for beer.

Captain Frederick Pabst can perhaps claim the lion's

share of credit for Milwaukee's status as a world-renowned brewing center. In 1893, the Captain became the first brewer in America to sell more than one million barrels of beer in a single year. (Though the majority was packaged in wood kegs, the brewery used 300,000 yards of blue ribbon each year to tie around the bottle necks of its popular Pabst Select brand. The name, of course, was later changed to Pabst Blue Ribbon.) By the turn-of-the-century, Pabst beer was being enjoyed in virtually every major city in the country.

That being the case, Captain Pabst undoubtedly took exception to competitor Schlitz's long-time slogan, "The Beer That Made Milwaukee Famous." In fact, Pabst snidely countered with a slogan of his own: "Milwaukee beer is famous—Pabst has made it so." Joseph Schlitz, however, may have gotten the final word in the rivalry. Before his tragic death during a shipwreck in the Atlantic in 1875, Schlitz had mandated in his will that his brewery never bear any name other than Schlitz. For more than one hundred years afterward, the two Milwaukee breweries battled for the top position among America's beermakers, both achieving great prosperity along the way.

The German Social Icon

No question: To the beer barons, beer meant wealth and success. However, to the countless German-American immigrants of the late-19th century, lager beer meant something far different. Lager beer was, perhaps more than anything else, a social icon. It represented family, friends, and German camaraderie. And nowhere was this more true than at the local beer garden. A weekend resort laid out amidst shady trees and sprawling lawns, the typical beer garden was manicured to be the perfect setting for that most important of 19th century pastimes: quaffing the amber fluid. And there was barely an American town in the mid- to late-1800s that did not boast one (or two, or three) of these beer drinking utopias.

After all, the beer garden provided something which most immigrant-Americans could not get anywhere else— something the Germans called *gemütlichkeit*. Near and dear to the heart of the average Teuton, *gemütlichkeit* was a sort of cozy, warm state of being created only by the presence of good friends, close family, a relaxing environment, and, more often than not, plenty of beer.

But the typical beer garden offered far more than just beer and *gemütlichkeit*. There was music, dancing, sport and leisure. It was an occasion for the whole family, and one which usually lasted the entire day, from sunup to sundown. Indeed, for the mostly working class throngs who came, the beer garden was an oasis in an otherwise workaday life. As such, it played an important role in the lives of countless immigrants.

Milwaukee, of course, was the undisputed leader in the number (and extravagance) of beer gardens. Competition between the city's dozens of gardens was fierce, and all manner of entertainment was employed to lure a large beer-drinking crowd. Lueddemann's Garden, for example, once featured a "daring and beautiful" female performer who set fire to herself and plunged 40 feet into the river below, much to the delight of on-lookers.

However, those gardens which were owned by the beer barons themselves featured the most popular attractions. In 1879, the Schlitz brewery bought a local beer garden and turned it into a magnificent resort, appropriately re-named Schlitz Park. The large garden was a virtual entertainment mecca, featuring a concert pavilion, a dance hall, a bowling alley, refreshment parlors, and live performers such as tightrope walkers and other circus-style entertainers. In the center of the park was a hill topped by a three-story pagoda-like structure which offered a panoramic view

of the city. At night, the garden was dramatically illumi-
nated by the 250 gas globes which lined the terrace of the
central hill. The park was a popular spot for political gatherings. Among those who made speeches at Schlitz Park
over the years were Grover Cleveland, William McKinley,
Theodore Roosevelt and William Jennings Bryan.

Not to be outdone by his hometown rival, Captain
Pabst operated Pabst Park in Milwaukee (among other
beer gardens). The eight-acre resort boasted a 15,000-foot-
long roller coaster, a "Katzenjammer palace" fun house,
and an oddity touted as "the smallest real railroad in the
world." Wild west shows were held on a regular basis, and
live orchestras performed seven days a week all through
summer. Of course, whatever the attraction, a 5¢ schooner
of cold Pabst Beer was never far from reach.

While both Schlitz and Pabst appealed to the more ad-
venturesome and thrill-seeking of Milwaukee's German
community, Frederick Miller's garden on the western out-
skirts of the city catered to a somewhat more reserved
clientele. A visitor to Miller's Garden wrote in 1873: "The
garden, situated on a lofty eminence, overlooking a wide
stretch of green and rolling country . . . is a very pleasing
place to while away the hours of a scorching afternoon.
Seated at a rustic table beneath leafy bowers, men and
women, staid and middle-aged, during pauses in their
friendly conversation, sipped their amber lager. In the spa-
cious pavilion, Clauder's band rendered sweet music."

Major Beer Properties

The Milwaukee beer barons did not, by any means, limit
their beer drinking spots to the confines of Milwaukee. The
Schlitz brewery, for instance, operated gardens and saloons
in major cities throughout the country. In Chicago alone,
Schlitz owned some sixty different properties around the
turn of the century. Captain Pabst, too, was a large holder

of saloons and restaurants outside Milwaukee. When the Captain decided to invade New York City, he did so in grand fashion, opening the Pabst Hotel in 1899 and the Pabst Harlem in 1900. Claiming to be the largest restaurant in America, the Pabst Harlem was capable of seating 1,400 patrons at once. It was said that the Captain hired famous New York stage actors to walk into the Harlem, order a beer, and say in a loud voice, "I am drinking to the health of Milwaukee's greatest beer brewer, Captain Fred Pabst."

The Barons' Undoing

Given that the beer barons of the late 19th and early 20th century sold their brew—and, thus, built their fortunes— almost exclusively through beer gardens and saloons, it is a little ironic that those very establishments ultimately contributed to their undoing. Historically speaking, the Prohibition movement in America targeted not the brewer, not the distiller, not even the drunkard, but rather the disreputable saloon—those urban "grogshops" where, according to the prohibitionists, prostitution and gambling ran wild. Indeed, far and away the most important force in bringing about National Prohibition (1920–1933) was the Anti-Saloon League. While the League's central goal was most certainly the complete destruction of the alcoholic beverage industry in America, its strategists believed that the saloon was the Achilles' heel which could bring victory to their cause. And, much to the dismay of the beer barons, the theory proved supremely effective in the end.

Although Prohibition put an abrupt end to what has been called "the golden age" of beermaking in America, vestiges of that era are still everywhere around us. The brewing industry, after all, is steeped in tradition like few other industries in America. Unusually strong rights of inheritance have kept many American breweries under the same familial management for generations. Brewers like

Anheuser-Busch, Miller, Coors, Pabst and others, while not all controlled by their founding families today, nevertheless carry a century-old legacy rooted in the Gilded Age prosperity of the German-American beer barons. So great was their influence on brewing in America that, more than a century later, their names live on in testament to their grand achievements.

CHAPTER 3

German Immigration During the 1900s

COMING TO AMERICA

Superpatriotism: Proving Loyalty to America During World War I

Frederick C. Luebke

The threat of war with Germany changed life significantly
for German Americans in 1917. America's imminent entry
into World War I resulted in what Frederick C. Luebke calls
"superpatriotism" on the part of both native Americans and
immigrants. In the following selection Luebke tells how German immigrants in particular had to go to extremes to prove
loyalty to their adopted country. Despite their superpatriotic
efforts, they often came under suspicion and were occasionally persecuted. The author is a retired professor of history
at the University of Nebraska, Lincoln. He is the author of
many books and articles on German immigrants, including
*Immigrants and Politics: The Germans of Nebraska,
1880–1900* and *Bonds of Loyalty: German-Americans and
World War I*, the source of this selection.

"Those were the sweetless, wheatless, meatless, heatless,
and perfectly brainless days when your fathers broke
Beethoven's records, boycotted Wagner's music, burned
German books, painted German Lutheran churches and
Goethe's monument in Chicago the color of Shell filling
stations today; strung up a Mennonite preacher in Collinsville, Oklahoma, by his neck until he fainted, repeated the

process until he fainted again, and graciously relented; hanged another to a limb of a tree in Collinsville, Illinois, until he was dead." So mused Oscar Ameringer, a German-born American Socialist, as he recalled the enthusiasm with which Americans fought World War I at home. He was describing the fruit of a trend, rooted in the prewar decade, which grew vigorously during the neutrality period and ripened after the declaration of war.

By no means were all Americans caught up in the hysteria of superpatriotism. Many were ambivalent in their own feelings about American involvement and could sympathize with the German-American in his predicament. During the first four or five months of the war a number of prominent public officials and journalists were explicit about their confidence in the loyalty of the Germans. Even President [Woodrow] Wilson, for example, wrote in August 1917:

> I have been made aware from various sources of the unfortunate position in which a very large number of our loyal fellow-citizens are placed because of their German origin or affiliations. I am sure that they need no further assurance from me of my confidence in the entire integrity and loyalty of the great body of our citizens of German blood.

Meanwhile the public and private agencies of propaganda delineated the new patriotism, and noisy bigots increasingly baited German-Americans. But most citizens preferring to accept ethnic protestations of loyalty at face value, adopted a wait-and-see attitude.

Varying Responses to the War

The millions of Americans of German birth or descent were anything but uniform in their response to war. The most obstinate among them insisted on displaying pictures of Kaiser Wilhelm as they had in the neutrality period, or refused to rise and sing the "Star-Spangled Banner" in public gatherings. Some were perhaps stupid; certainly they were indiscreet. A German farmer in Kansas flew the German flag above his home; an Indiana man muttered insults as he ripped a likeness of President Wilson from the wall. Others were merely tactless or naïve. In Chicago, a city where sixty alleged leaders of pro-German propaganda had been arrested almost simultaneously with the declaration of war, a group of German Lutheran clergymen met to make plans for serving the young men from their churches who would soon be drafted into the armed forces. They conducted their sessions in the German language and called themselves the Evangelische Lutherische Missions behoerde fuer Heer und Flotte, as they prepared to deal with the national government. Fortunately, a fellow pastor in Washington, D.C., convinced them of the need to translate the name to the Lutheran Army and Navy Board.

At the opposite end of the spectrum were German-Americans who embraced all the tenets of superpatriotism. They hoped to shed all marks of German ethnicity and were severely critical of persons and institutions that, in their opinion, inhibited assimilation. A variety of associations were organized to accomplish the conformists' goals. In New York, for example, a group founded a society to implement an advertiser's boycott of German-language newspapers. Other similar organizations sprang up across the country to establish the absolute loyalty of the Germans in America. In Chicago a group of German Lutheran laymen formed the American Lutheran Patriotic League. On a broader scale there was the National Patriotic Council of Americans of German Origin, a large association that was backed by Secretary of the Interior Franklin K. Lane. The most highly publicized organization was the Friends of German Democracy. Really a propaganda agency sponsored by the Committee on Public Information, it distributed much literature denouncing the Hohenzollern [the ruling family] autocracy and calling for the creation of a German republic. . . .

Objects of Suspicion

Most Germans in America held attitudes somewhere between the pro-German and superloyalist extremes. Like most Americans they regretted that war had to come but there was no question in their minds about meeting their responsibilities as citizens. Although they were fearful of the domestic consequences of war, they were psychologically unprepared to cope with the myriad ways in which superpatriotism affected mundane aspects of their lives. Most experienced feelings akin to those described by Theodore Ladenburger, a German Jewish merchant of New York who had emigrated from Germany twenty-five years earlier. Ladenburger had exulted in his success in America and although he retained an emotional attachment for Germany, he had agreed strongly that American entry into the European conflict was appropriate and just. Yet, he wrote,

> From the moment that the United States had declared war on Germany, I was made to feel the pinpricks of an invisible but so much more hurtful and pernicious ostracism as a traitor to my adopted country. I had never looked for sympathy in my bewildering dilemma. But in view of my record as a citizen I did not expect from my neighbors and fellow citizens a fair estimate and appreciation of my honesty and trustworthiness. It had all vanished. Outstanding was only the fact, of which I was never ashamed—nor did I ever make a secret of it—that I had been born in Germany.

Thus Ladenburger and innumerable other German-Americans tended to perceive themselves as objects of suspicion, innocent victims of whispered lies, citizens whose distinguished records of civic virtue were ignored or for-

gotten, whose private lives were subjected to unfair investigation, and whose deeds were condemned without a hearing or judged disloyal unless proven otherwise. They were
sensitive, as never before, to the slightest slur, the knowing glance, the condescending remark. But native-born, established Americans regarded the status of German-born
citizens in a society at war with Germany rather differently.
They considered themselves to be tolerant of German-
Americans and understanding of the emotional stress imposed by the war. They agreed that the great majority were
firmly loyal, but that it was only fair to judge the German-
Americans by their deeds, especially because of their apparently pro-German behavior during the neutrality period. Americans naturally wanted to analyze every word
uttered by their German-born neighbors and scrutinize
every action taken by ethnic organizations for evidence of
disloyalty, sedition, and treason.

Hopes for a Speedy Victory

From the first days of the war, most German-language
newspapers gave the superpatriots little cause for alarm. In
general, they closed ranks quickly behind President Wilson, declaring their unequivocal loyalty and printing edito-
rials counseling subscribers to do their patriotic duty and
to avoid giving offense. There was also much superficial display of patriotism. Front pages were splashed with American flags, national anthems, and patriotic poetry; editors
gave advertising space to war bond drives, patriotic meetings, and appeals for contributions to the Red Cross and the
YMCA. This was more than cynical or expedient submis-
sion to popular demands for conformity. During the neutrality period, they, like many other Americans, had insisted that the United States would best be served by
avoiding war; but now they saw no alternative to working
for the speedy victory of American arms over Germany.

A few German-American editors, however, found the transition painful. A Seattle paper, for example, denounced the declaration of war as a national catastrophe brought about by "British gold, Wall Street, ammunition makers, and the indifference of the people." More caustically, the *New Haven Anzeiger* observed that everything in this world has an end; bologna even has two ends, but "stupidity alone is without end and without limit." Some papers cast their patriotism in terms that permitted them to nourish hatred for England. According to the *Cincinnati Volksblatt*, "To support the United States is a duty. To support the President as the representative of the United States is no less a duty; but to have to support England, that hypocritical robber nation, that hereditary enemy of our country, that's what makes one heartsick." Others hoped that somehow the war might end before the United States became fully engaged in the fighting. Still others tried to avoid editorial comment on the questions raised by American involvement and limited themselves to straight reporting of war news. Not a few German-American editors believed that Germany would win in any case. Hence, they liked to give reports of German victories prominent placement on their front pages. By the end of summer, however, most German-American intransigents had so modified their stance that their publications had become vehicles of patriotic propaganda. . . .

Concerns About the Draft

A few die-hards anguished over conscription. George Sylvester Viereck, for example, contended that draftees of German origin should be excused from fighting in France. There were many other avenues of service, he argued, without being forced to fire upon one's kinsmen. A few papers repeated Viereck's arguments and a number of petitions were sent to Congress urging amendments to the draft law which would favor German-Americans. Basically, however, this seems to have been an elitist concern not founded on widespread sentiment. Except for Socialists and those who objected for religious reasons, German-Americans responded to the draft as willingly as any group in America. Only in New Ulm, Minnesota, where antiwar feelings were nourished by a few intransigent leaders, was there a major ethnic demonstration against conscription. It was obvious to almost all other German-American spokesmen that such behavior gave substance to charges of ethnic disloyalty. Hence, nearly all German-language newspapers urged full compliance with the law and explained its detailed requirements for the benefit of readers whose comprehension of English was limited.

The advent of war presented insuperable difficulties for the thousands of organizations whose objectives were closely related to the maintenance of German culture. In general, they sought to remain as inconspicuous as possible and refrained from drawing attention to themselves by formal declarations or public activities. The National German-American Alliance, however, because of its prominence, followed an explicitly patriotic course. It issued a call to all members to meet every responsibility imposed by citizenship. Although it was subsequently accused of dilatory patriotism, the alliance took much pride in its participation in the several Liberty bond drives. Absolute loyalty to the United States was a constant theme in its literature, as was the requirement of proper conduct. But the various alliances understandably hesitated to display sympathy for America's allies and they were less than eager to publicly condemn Germany's war aims or to blame the war on the Kaiser, as the superpatriots demanded.

A few local German-American organizations responded to the declaration of war with dramatic gestures. An association of New York societies offered its shooting range and park in New Jersey to the War Department. The Germania Club of Jacksonville, Florida, offered the facilities of its new $100,000 clubhouse to the Red Cross free of charge. But these were exceptions. The behavior of the Cincinnati Alliance was typical of many more of the vereins [social-ethnic clubs]. Like the national organization, it quickly declared its loyalty, organized itself for the sale of war bonds, and supported Red Cross activities. Its officers exhorted members to destroy German flags, to remove pictures of the Kaiser and his generals, and to stop trying to send money and gifts to relatives in Germany. Its members scrupulously avoided discussing the war as the organization returned to its traditional interest in state and local issues—prohibition, woman suffrage, and school affairs.

Ethnic organizations whose purposes were ideological, unlike the social and cultural vereins, resisted pressure to conform to wartime standards of patriotic behavior. This was especially true of the Socialists. Their newspapers, both in the English and German languages, boldly attacked the declaration of war as a crime against the American people, intended to safeguard Wall Street investments and disguised in lofty but hypocritical rhetoric. Shortly before American entry, the executive committee of the Socialist party called for an emergency convention in Saint Louis on 7 April 1917 to forge a wartime program. Reaffirming their allegiance to international working class solidarity against capitalist exploitation, the Socialists resolved to stand firm in their opposition to the war, conscription, press censorship, and all restrictions of free speech. The Saint Louis manifesto aroused the apostles of conformity to storms of denunciation. Except for a splinter group of Anglo-Americans who endorsed the war, most Socialists were then excoriated as pro-German traitors, The *New York World*, for example, declared that there was no longer any room for the Socialist party in the United States because it was almost wholly a

German product working for a German victory. Before long
Socialist newspapers were subjected to much harassment
and many fell under the ban of censorship.

Churches Faced Peculiar Problems

American entry into the war created a problem of peculiar
dimensions for the German-American churches. None of
them had had formal or institutional ties with Germany,
much less the German government; indeed, many church
Germans had emigrated in protest to the religious policies
of German states. They took their own allegiance to the
United States for granted, something above question.
While they continued to place high value on their ethnocultural heritage, they believed it to be unrelated to the war
and devoid of genuine political implications. Hence, they
could make declarations of loyalty freely and without
reservation, unnecessary though they seemed. During
April and May the leaders of nearly all German-American
denominations contributed to the flood of loyalty pledges.
They said that the citizen who had once pleaded for peace
would now render faithful service, as befits a Christian.
Willingness to work and fight, however, was not tanta-
mount to approval of war in general as a means of national
policy, or of this war in particular as being in the best interest of the United States. Nor were they willing to equate
patriotic service with modifying their use of German language and culture. They believed that they had every right
to continue using German in their worship services,
schools, business meetings, and publications. Naturally,
this stance made the German churches easy targets of war-
born chauvinism. Unlike most of the vereins, which readily faded under superpatriotic pressure, the churches tried
in 1917 to maintain a "business-as-usual" policy.

Some German-American churchmen quickly recognized
that the times demanded positive action in order to prevent

further erosion of their status in American society. In contrast to those who remained aloof, they sought appointments to local councils of defense, to Red Cross and Liberty bond drive committees, or as Four Minute speakers. Others freely violated their liturgical sensibilities by displaying the American flag in their sanctuaries and by having their congregations sing the "Star-Spangled Banner."

Advocates of such measures were usually assimilationists who were seeking to Americanize their churches. Often identified as theological liberals, they believed that the church's mission demanded a rapid transition to the English language, that the church should become thoroughly involved in patriotic activities, and that this involvement should be widely publicized, thereby defending the church against unfounded charges of disloyalty. Conservatives, by contrast, tended to ignore the demands made upon them by the superpatriots. The church was apolitical, they insisted; to abandon the German language would inhibit the church's responsibility to preach the Gospel; to permit patriotic speechmaking in the church would dilute its message; to indulge in patriotic display would violate the boundary between church and state and cheapen both in the process. Confident in their loyalty, conservatives hoped to weather the storm by retreating still further into their ethnic shells.

In general, German-Americans of all kinds were bewildered by the onset of war. Since the test of loyalty rested in superficial behavior, they were expected to declare their allegiance with great fervor, to work vigorously and sacrificially for victory over Germany, and to reject German ethnocultural elements of their identity. If they remained silent on the subject of the war or assented passively to it, as most of them did, they were likely to be charged with lukewarm patriotism. If they conformed enthusiastically to the new standards, they could be charged, as some were, with making a show of patriotism to mask their essential disloyalty.

Fleeing Hitler: The German Cultural Elite Come to America

Jarrell C. Jackman

During the rise of the Nazi regime in Germany in the 1930s, Adolf Hitler was convinced that education should be devoted to developing healthy bodies and mental discipline. He believed that cultural and intellectual pursuits led to weak minds and bodies ill-prepared for the rigors of his new society. As a result, many of the country's cultural elite—composers, musicians, writers, and artists—were persecuted and forced to flee to other countries. In the following selection, Jarrell C. Jackman describes how some of these German immigrants fared when they settled in Southern California to work in Hollywood. In particular, he explains how their feelings of cultural superiority made it difficult for them to adjust to their new lives. The author, a former lecturer in history at the University of Maryland, is currently the executive director of the Santa Barbara Trust for Historic Preservation.

In January 1980 I spent an evening with the émigré Marta Feuchtwanger at her home in Pacific Palisades [California]. We stood on the terrace looking out at the ocean under a starry sky—a scene most serene and beautiful. Other guests were present that evening, all of us captivated by the setting, all of us aware that this once had been a center of ex-

Jarrell C. Jackman, "German Émigrés in Southern California," *The Muses Flee Hitler: Cultural Transfer and Adaptation, 1930–1945*, edited by Jarrell C. Jackman and Carla M. Borden. Washington, DC: Smithsonian Institution Press, 1983. Copyright © 1983 by the Smithsonian Institution. All rights reserved. Reproduced by permission of the author.

ile activity: the home where the novelist Lion Feuchtwanger entertained émigrés during the 1940s. Still clear-minded at ninety-one, full of life and memories, Mrs. Feuchtwanger is living history; she enjoys showing her deceased husband's extensive collection of books, each one of them with a story behind it, many of them rare first editions and inscribed copies by fellow émigrés such as [writer] Thomas Mann.

In this castle-by-the-sea one cannot help but ask the question: is this what exile was like in southern California? If so, can this even be called "exile," and how typical was it of the émigré experience? After spending an afternoon at Feuchtwanger's, the émigré author Herman Kesten left amazed by what he had seen: a twenty-room Spanish-style home with a view of the mountains and ocean; all kinds of fruit trees; a garden filled with flowers; a park with benches and breakfast tables. As Kesten said, "What a life!" It undoubtedly had its comforts, and there must have been occasions when Feuchtwanger thought to himself that all the troubles he had had to endure in escaping the Nazis were worthwhile—if this was the end result.

But, of course, the end result was not the same for all the émigrés. While Feuchtwanger lived in luxury, writers such as Heinrich Mann, Alfred Döblin, and Bertolt Brecht struggled to eke out an existence in their small bungalows and apartments. Employed by the film studios as scriptwriters, they had to bear the full brunt of adapting to a new life in a strange and frightening world. In some cases they were too old to learn English and too set in their ways to interact with the new environment. They had not been interested in America, nor had they had an audience for their works here, before emigrating—in contrast to Feuchtwanger.

So they arrived in southern California, unprepared for what they encountered. That the region is located at one of the westernmost points of the New World is important because, as individuals steeped in their Old World culture, they traveled almost the length of Western civilization, across the Atlantic Ocean, then clear across the continental United States, with each mile separating them further from the Old World and its cultural traditions. They had to adapt to a warm environment after the cold and bracing climate of Germany. They glimpsed a new cultural landscape filled with bungalows spread across the vast Los Angeles basin, and connected by highways swarming with automobiles. On the streets they saw Californians dressed casually, wearing short-sleeved shirts and knickers [short pants]. In the studios they witnessed a hyperactive, frantic business world. Everywhere they looked they saw evidence that this was the New World, and they experienced a real sense of being cut off from their past.

Attitudes and Adaptation

How well the émigrés adapted to this new environment depended in part on their attitudes toward southern California. If an émigré viewed himself as the standard bearer of "high culture" and southern California as "lowbrow," then there were bound to be some problems.

Such was the case with the émigré composer Arnold Schoenberg, who was often appalled by what he saw in southern California. He wrote, at one point, to [artist] Oskar Kokoschka in New York:

> You complain of lack of culture in this amusement-arcade world [of America]. I wonder what you'd say to the world in which I nearly die of disgust. I don't only mean the "movies." Here is an advertisement by way of example: There's a picture of a man who has run over a child, which is lying dead in front of his car. He clutches his head in despair, but not to say anything like: "My God, what have I done?" For there is a caption saying: "Sorry, now it is too late to worry—take out your policy at the XX Insurance Company in time." And these are the people I'm supposed to teach composition to!

The local hedonistic mass society so offended his German sensibilities that Schoenberg could not help believing that "everything was all wrong" in Los Angeles, and while the local residents could be very "kind and helpful," he found them "mostly inferior." He did not want to be influenced by this world and rejected the notion that the physical environment had affected him: "If immigration has changed me," he wrote, "I am unaware of it. Maybe I would have written more when remaining in Europe, but I think: nothing comes out what was not in [sic]. And two times two equals four in every climate."

Schoenberg received his inspiration from the German classical music tradition in which he fervently believed. That was the main reason for his feeling so strongly about his work as well as for his reacting so bitterly to the world of southern California. But, of course, Schoenberg was always the temperamental genius and had previously bemoaned the lack of recognition he had received in Europe. His music, too controversial for many conductors and composers and too dissonant for the conventional tastes of listeners, was never performed enough to satisfy him. In Los Angeles the same proved true: Schoenberg complained that, "Mr. Wallenstein [conductor of the Los Angeles Philharmonic] is here six years . . . and has not yet played one piece of mine."

This hurt not only his artistic pride, but his pocketbook. After retiring from teaching composition at the University of California at Los Angeles, Schoenberg was financially insecure. Still, he could not bring himself to write music for Hollywood films. This would have been selling out and beneath him. And who is to say he was wrong in making the choice he did? The fact was, he became bitter about his situation and wrote:

> there will certainly be in perhaps twenty years a chapter in the musical history of Los Angeles: "What Schoenberg has achieved in Los Angeles"; and perhaps there will

be another chapter, asking: "What have the people and the society of Los Angeles taken of the advantage offered by Schoenberg?". . .

Immigrant Musicians in Hollywood

Those émigrés who worked in the studios were, for the most part, well-educated, serious musicians representing high culture, while the people they worked for were usually men of little education who produced films for popular consumption. As members of the German cultural elite, the émigrés were accustomed to being treated with a certain amount of respect, but found themselves frequently insulted by their Hollywood bosses.

Friedrich Hollander described in his autobiography some of the problems with which he had to contend. Initially he was hired by Twentieth-Century-Fox, where he was given his own office with a piano; he was then approached by a producer who asked him to score a film, which he did, and which became a successful movie. Hollander's mistake, though, was not asking his department head for permission to do the score. Even though the music and the movie were well received, Hollander was fired for not having gone through proper channels.

Later, however, he was hired by Paramount, and again given an assignment. His film score was played through for several executives, the composer waiting anxiously in the wings for their reaction. After a long silence at the end of the movie, one of the executives stood up and said: "Piss in ice water." Aghast, Hollander stood there dazed, certain his Hollywood career was over. Then someone else added that it was not really so bad, and the group decided to use the score without any changes. The upshot of this incident was that the very man who had reacted so crudely to his first work did more than anyone else to promote Hollander's Hollywood career. Hollander and most of the émigré composers learned to expect the unexpected, and with a healthy check coming in every week, they swallowed their pride and did the work assigned. The émigrés ended up making a major contribution to the scoring of films (in some cases, their music being the only redeeming quality of the movies they worked on).

Resentment Grew Among Writers

The great advantage the émigré composers and musicians had over writers and actors was not being bound to language for economic survival. Except for Schoenberg, the émigré composers were also more positive in their attitudes toward southern California than were most of the writers, who did a great deal of moaning and groaning about Hollywood and cultureless Californians, even though many of them had been given one-year contracts as scriptwriters. This grousing is understandable considering some of their situations as exiles. What should be kept in mind is that there has been a long line of American and European writers who have come away from Hollywood disgusted by the experience. The letters and diaries of Bertolt Brecht, Leonhard Frank, and a number of other émigrés are replete with snide and angry comments about Hollywood and southern California. These men, like Schoenberg, considered themselves artists and representatives of "German culture," and they resented being told what to create.

They resented, too, being cut down to size by Americans they felt were their intellectual inferiors. That happened to the émigré Frederick Kohner the first time he met Harry Cohn, president of Columbia Studios. Kohner wanted to thank Cohn for hiring him, and when shown into the president's office, he expressed his gratitude. Cohn growled back that if Kohner did not produce he would be "kicked in the pants" out the door. Kohner, having earned a Ph.D. in Europe, felt affronted; as he got up to leave, Cohn told the "Herr Doktor" [Lord Doctor] that he had better get used to the way people talked in Hollywood. He did eventually and decided that the money made this life bearable, an attitude also shared by a number of émigré writers, some of whom made lasting contributions to the Hollywood film industry. Among the most famous was Billy Wilder, who began as a scriptwriter and later directed *Sunset Boulevard* and *Lost Weekend*, two of the finest movies to come out of Hollywood in the 1940s and 1950s.

Frederick Kohner also made his mark in Hollywood, as a scriptwriter and later as a novelist. One of the more interesting facts of the German immigration to southern California is that the émigré Kohner wrote in English the novel *Gidget* (1957), which in addition to selling millions of copies in America and abroad was made into a successful movie and television series. The novel portrays the southern California surfer world, in which what mattered most was one's suntan. The favorite pastimes of Gidget's friends were "shooting the breeze," "making out," "tooling down the main drag," "getting annihilated on beer," or "fractured on wine," to quote some of the phrases used in the novel. These were the activities of young teenagers totally oblivious to anything except their hedonistic lifestyle. Having raised a daughter in this environment, Kohner cashed in on being able to capture the experience in his novel, and he lives today [in 1983] a rather affluent life in his Brentwood home.

Several other émigré writers also achieved a similar level of affluence. In the 1940s, Bruno Frank, Franz Werfel, Thomas Mann and Lion Feuchtwanger bought homes in Beverly Hills or Pacific Palisades. Frank, Werfel, and Feuchtwanger wrote for or sold stories to Hollywood, but Mann depended on the royalties from his works in translation and the salary he received as a consultant to the Library of Congress on German literature.

There was considerable contact between these men, who also hobnobbed with some of the important names in Hollywood. The interaction between the Germans and the Americans remained generally informal, and the intellectual impact they had on one another was minimal. The Germans depended on one another for intellectual stimulation because of common interests in politics and cultural matters. In a few cases, living in southern California did influence their writings. Feuchtwanger, for example, wrote a short story on Venice, California, a beach community south of Pacific Palisades, and Werfel's last novel, *Star of the Unborn*, has some descriptions of life in Beverly Hills. Yet, for the most part, the émigrés continued to write their fictional works on subjects relating to Germany or Europe, while limiting their reactions to southern California to letters and diaries. The most extreme example of this was Thomas Mann, who lived more than ten years in southern California and wrote nothing about America in his fiction. The only American influence he could attribute to his novel *Joseph the Provider* (1943) was that it had been written under "the Egyptian-like sky of California.". . .

Bitterness Set In

Among the émigrés it would be difficult to find anyone more bitter than [poet and dramatist Carl] Zuckmayer. From the day he arrived in southern California, he felt alienated from his surroundings, especially in Hollywood where he lived and worked. He became so unnerved by the frantic pace inside the studios that he insisted on staying home to do his scriptwriting. But he could not escape the world outside the studios, which also struck him as chaotic. The women in stores and restaurants seemed plastic and made up like dolls; they chewed gum incessantly while awaiting the big moment of discovery by some movie mogul. After only a few months in Hollywood, Zuckmayer decided he had better return to New York before he went mad. Of his last day in southern California, he wrote:

> I saw Hollywood one last time in all its horror. Artificial Christmas trees with electric candles in all imaginable colors, chiefly pink, orange, and silvery blue, stood in front of the houses. I had been invited to a party given in the Beverly Hills Hotel. A slide had been covered with artificial snow and men in bathing trunks, women in silk jerseys, skied down it directly into the cocktail tent. Huge crimson poinsettias bloomed in all the gardens. The sight of all this nauseated me.

Zuckmayer had not been very successful as a screen-writer, but it would leave a false impression to conclude that those who succeeded in Hollywood did not complain, while those who failed did complain. There were several well-paid émigré scriptwriters, including Curt Goetz, as well as other writers not dependent on Hollywood, who found southern California a mind-boggling experience. Erich Maria Remarque, for example, recorded how the people on a southern California beach affected him:

> Unemployed extras were strutting about, hoping to be discovered by a talent scout. The waitresses in the restaurants and snack bars were all waiting for the great moment, meanwhile consuming lavish quantities of make-up, tight-fitting pants and short skirts. The whole place was one giant lottery: Who would pick the winning number? Who would be discovered for the movies?

There have been so many lines like this written about Hollywood and southern California that it would have been surprising had the émigrés not chimed in with their criticisms. While the émigrés themselves can be criticized for their ingratitude to Hollywood, which, after all, had literally saved some of their lives by providing them with jobs in the studios, their anger is understandable in light of the traumas most of them had gone through as exiles. Their egos had been substantially deflated in southern California, where the local denizens had very little interest in German culture. In fact, Germany was the enemy that America, after 1941, was intent on destroying, and it would have seemed a contradiction in terms—at least to the popular mind—to be interested in preserving German culture in America. . . .

And what happened to the many . . . émigré actors who ended up in Hollywood? To their good fortune, after 1941, Hollywood began producing a series of anti-Nazi films and employed the German actors, whose accents were perfect for the parts. Another irony of the German emigration was the casting of these émigré actors as Nazis, their archenemies. . . .

A Cultural Boost for America

The German exile experience in southern California ran the gamut between sheer agony and pleasant living. The Germans were fortunate in having so many of their fellow countrymen around them, so that if they could not adapt to certain conditions in exile, they at least had someone with whom to commiserate. But in the world of southern California, they had to learn to accept what they encountered or suffer the economic consequences. Sometimes they did a little too much "nose-thumbing" and could be ridiculously arrogant in their attitude toward America. It helped if the émigré had a positive feeling for his home in exile, but this did not guarantee ultimate success.

The ability of the émigrés to assimilate into the cultural life of southern California was determined by a set of factors: age, facility in English, profession, temperament, and attitude toward his home in exile. On the whole, it can be said that most were able to assimilate—as teachers in local universities, as musicians and composers, as novelists, as movie actors, directors, and screenwriters. At the same time, southern California allowed the Germans to intermingle freely and in the process guaranteed that a certain amount of their culture would be preserved. Today there are archives containing émigré manuscripts and other material at the Universities of California at Santa Barbara and Los Angeles and at the University of Southern California. Through these archives a part of German culture survives in the region, as does an academic interest in the émigrés' years in Los Angeles. . . .

While there is still much research to be undertaken, from our present historical vantage point we can begin to understand the significance of the German immigration to southern California in the 1930s and 1940s. On one level, it provided a boost to the cultural life of the region, illustrating once again the ability of America to absorb other cultures and to benefit from them. On another level, the German migration bridged two cultures separated by thousands of miles. What resulted was an interaction between the émigrés, who represented an Old World culture dating back centuries, and southern California, a New World future-oriented region. It appeared on the surface that these two forces were irreconcilable—the Germans bound to the past, the southern Californians forward-looking. But in actuality the threads connecting them became strong, and an actual cultural synthesis took place when the émigrés composed for Hollywood, when Frederick Kohner wrote his novels, and when Walter Wicclair staged his plays. But still something was lost—a number of careers were ruined and full advantage was not taken of the émigrés by the region. Such was the price to be paid for Hitler's expulsion of the German cultural elite.

A return to Marta Feuchtwanger's terrace in Pacific Palisades is a fitting place and way to conclude this essay. Outside on that terrace once stood Thomas Mann, Bertolt Brecht, and numerous other important German intellectual figures of the twentieth century, and from that terrace they could look out over the Pacific Ocean with the blue sky above. Externally, all appeared calm and serene, but internally the émigrés were caldrons of emotions. Their hearts were laden with past painful experiences; they could not forget the turn of events that had uprooted and transplanted them to America. Yet, for all their personal problems and the difficulties they faced in working for Hollywood, one is left with the impression that the émigrés had been rather fortunate in being exiled in the Lotus Land of southern California.

Nazi Activity Among German Americans Before World War II

Timothy J. Holian

The vast majority of German Americans were horrified by the rise of the Nazis and their activities in Germany before the outbreak of World War II. Nevertheless, in the early 1930s a small number of Nazi sympathizers in the United States tried to generate support for Adolf Hitler and his Nazi regime. In the following selection Timothy J. Holian describes how the entire German American community came under suspicion because of the deeds of a few Nazi organizers. The author also explains how the American public and the U.S. government tried to quell the American Nazi groups' activities. These organizations eventually lost support with the onset of the war and its atrocities. Holian is an associate professor of German at Missouri Western State College. He is the author of *Over the Barrel: The Brewing History and Beer Culture of Cincinnati* and *The German-Americans and World War II: An Ethnic Experience*, from which the following selection is excerpted.

In order to understand the rationale behind American distrust of the German element in the United States, it is first necessary to examine the factors contributing to the changing perception of German aliens and the German American community. More than any other factor during the mid- to late 1930s, the rise of Nazism in Germany and the

Timothy J. Holian, *The German-Americans and World War II: An Ethnic Experience.* New York: Peter Lang Publishing, 1998. Copyright © 1996 by Peter Lang Publishing, Inc. All rights reserved. Reproduced by permission.

growth of pro-Nazi German organizations in America played a role in creating distrust of German legal resident aliens and German-Americans. Though the vast number of such members of the German-American community were loyal to American interests, and anti-Nazi in their sentiments, the actions of a small but vocal minority of pro-Nazi German legal resident aliens and German-Americans brought about resentment and distrust towards the German-American community as a whole, reminiscent of the anti-German hysteria of World War I. Many loyal German-Americans were placed in the awkward position of guilt by association; this initial development of an anti-German sentiment would contribute to a later situation, in which German legal resident aliens and German-Americans would have to prove their innocence, despite a lack of evidence of wrongdoing.

Most Immigrants Were Repelled by Nazism

For the vast majority of Americans, and indeed German-Americans, Nazism as a philosophy was repugnant by nature. By the 1930s, racial discrimination attracted only a fringe group of fanatics, generally of low education and social levels. Images of a class-based society, led by an ethnically pure, superior race struck at the base of American beliefs and experiences: Most Americans were keenly aware that their forefathers had come to this country on immigrant ships, in search of a better life, in forming the multiethnic society known as the United States.

Pro-Nazi German legal resident aliens and German-Americans, hoping for support from other members of the German-American community, failed to realize that times had changed for the German element in America. In the wake of the anti-German hysteria of World War I, the German-American community was reluctant to assert any connection to Germany, political or otherwise; recalling the

public image of the Kaiser in World War I, the vast majority of German-Americans were not inclined to promote
Adolf Hitler as an ambassador of German politics or culture. A new course of isolationism had taken root with the
rapid postwar assimilation of the German element, most
notably in the core of German America, the Midwest.
Post–World War I immigration restrictions illustrated post-
war xenophobic attitudes, ultimately restricting the number of Germans able to come to the United States, and influencing the willingness of the German-American
community to give expression to its German character.
Three separate laws were passed, in 1921, 1924, and 1929,
which provided a limit of 150,000 immigrants per year
from countries located outside of the Western Hemisphere.
While Germany still received a relatively large quota, determined by an already large German stock within the country, immigration possibilities were still restricted for those
Germans wishing to come. In 1930, some 1,600,000 native-
born Germans resided in the United States; of those, two-
thirds had arrived before World War I. By 1930, there were
some seven million Americans of German stock, but of
them over seventy-five percent had been born in the United
States; the 600,000 post–World War I German immigrants
constituted a fraction of the United States' total population
of 124 million. What immigration did exist into the 1930s
was decisively interrupted when Hitler came to power in
1933, soon prohibited save for exceptional circumstances.

Such changes in the German-American community
went unnoticed by the majority of Americans, especially
with the rise of pro-Nazi groups in the wake of Hitler's as-
cension to power in Germany in 1933. Despite the fact that
only a few thousand German legal resident aliens and
German-Americans, out of the millions in the United
States, took an active role in pro-Nazi organizations and
their activities, the sight of members of America's German

community wearing uniforms and parading on behalf of National Socialism brought back memories of pro-Kaiser activities in the German-American community during the World War I era. This prompted calls from concerned citizens and groups, including veterans' organizations such as the American Legion and the Veterans of Foreign Wars, for monitoring, and stricter control over, German-American organizations, particularly those known or suspected to have connections to the Berlin government. In Cincinnati, as in other centers of German-American population, pro-Nazi organizations such as the Friends of New Germany and the German-American Bund came under close scrutiny from numerous sources, including local Jewish groups and veterans' organizations; and traditional activities such as German Day were monitored with increasing frequency, in an effort to monitor pro-Nazi organizations and identify those members of Cincinnati's German-American community who may have held pro-Nazi sympathies. While leaders in the German-American community attempted to differentiate the vast majority of its members, unsympathetic to Hitler and the goals of National Socialism, from Bundists and other pro-Nazi German legal resident aliens and German-Americans, their efforts met with only limited success. Congressional hearings on un-American activities kept the image of Nazi sympathizers fresh in the public consciousness, and sensationalized reports of Nazi espionage and sabotage groups served to undermine the credible efforts of German-Americans to show that they overwhelmingly supported American interests, and would not side with Hitler in the event of German hostilities with the United States.

Early Nazi Activities in the United States

As early as 1923, proponents of Nazism were in America, seeking to advance their philosophy in German communities in various parts of the country. One of the first spokesmen for Nazism in the United States was Kurt Georg Wilhelm Ludecke, who came to America under the instruction of Adolf Hitler in the early 1920s. His mission was fairly straightforward, namely to recruit members among German nationals for a proposed Nazi party. Ludecke's efforts met with only minimal success. He operated independently of the Nazi party in Germany and without sanction from the German government, and received no financial support from Germany for his efforts.

Before the end of the decade, another figure took the lead in attempts to organize a Nazi movement in the United States. Fritz Gissibl, a prominent Chicago Nazi sympathizer, organized an independent cell of storm troopers; the group, known as *Teutonia*, was incorporated under Illinois state law and was even sanctioned by the Nazi party in Germany. By 1932, it had established local organizations in New York, Detroit, Milwaukee, Boston, Philadelphia, Chicago, Los Angeles, and Cincinnati; membership grew primarily through word-of-mouth advertising and correspondence, though the effects of the Great Depression also contributed substantially to membership increases at the time. By June of the same year, the *Teutonia* group, after joining ranks with others in a rival faction known as "Gau-USA," became known as the Nazi Party, U.S.A., and Ludecke was formally declared official representative of the Nazi party in the United States.

Seven months later, though, when Adolf Hitler became Chancellor of Germany on January 30, 1933, American resistance to the existence of a Nazi party in America brought the group's aims into question among a greater scope of the American populace. In April, Berlin took the formal step of ordering all Nazi cells in the United States dissolved, in an effort to promote a positive public image. The young Nazi government, realizing the need to court a larger audience over time and gain a more positive image abroad, chose to step back and regroup rather than risk more permanent damage to its reputation and movement. Thus the *Teutonia*/Gau-USA group passed into history, although the ideology behind the movement, and its key figures, would soon return to prominence in American Nazi circles.

Consequently, another, less known figure, Heinz Spanknoebel, was given charge of planning and coordinating a new organization which would be the successor to the Nazi Party, U.S.A. Spanknoebel had previously headed the *Teutonia* organization in Detroit, and was now being charged with responsibility for asserting a Nazi presence in America, involving fellow German nationals in strategic locations around the country while building up a favorable reputation for Nazism and the German element among a larger cross-section of the American population.

The Friends of New Germany

The organization which Spanknoebel created became the first notable Nazi venture in the United States. Known formally as the *Bund der Freunde des neuen Deutschlands*, or "Friends of New Germany," the group came into being by the middle of 1933, and was recognized by several of the highest-ranking Nazis in Berlin. Specifically, Rudolf Hess [Hitler's deputy führer] assured Spanknoebel and other members of the organization that the Friends of New Germany would be the official Nazi organization throughout North America.

However, as word of the new Nazi group spread beyond the boundaries of the German community, public outcry again forced the Nazi element to pursue damage control measures; according to [author] Susan Canedy, "America, noting the growing Nazi menace in Germany and mindful of World War I experiences with German fifth columns, real and imagined, demanded the early policing of the movement." The Friends was established as a militaristic and openly anti-Semitic organization; its lack of cover for its intentions left it wide open to attack from virtually all segments of mainstream America. Giving little thought to how most Americans would react to his message, Spanknoebel crossed the country, speaking of the need to "clean up America" from racial amalgamation and corrupting Jewish influences. Not unpredictably, the group found itself under attack at most of Spanknoebel's stops.

Further negative publicity for the Friends was inevitable, as stories began to circulate of violence at Friends' rallies and meetings. The most notorious incident involving anti-Friends violence took place in Irvington, New Jersey, near Newark, on May 21, 1934, as a mob of some 1,000 anti-Nazi demonstrators raided a Friends meeting attended by seventy-five uniformed members. The attack, described as "vicious" by a reporter on the scene, injured more than fifteen persons, with two of them taken to the hospital for head lacerations, while thirty-five of the attackers were arrested. Fighting began literally the moment the uniformed Friends members arrived in their buses, as two cars pulled up alongside the buses, their occupants jumping out and beginning the melee, soon to be joined by hundreds of streetside protesters. Hoping to find sanctuary inside the hall, Friends members managing to enter found themselves surrounded on all sides by even more protesters, likewise pummeled by the mob as police reinforcements were called in. As members of the Friends of New Germany became scarcer, the mob began to turn on assembled newspaper reporters and cameramen, smashing cameras, tearing clothing, and blackening eyes in the process. Upon arrival of reinforcements from the Newark Police Department, an hour's worth of street fighting was finally brought under control, and the inside disturbances quelled, though upon withdrawal of the police forces from the auditorium the mob resumed its attack, launching an avalanche of bricks through second-story windows. Remaining Friends members were left abandoned when their bus drivers, alarmed by the violence as well as several well-placed stench bombs, deserted them by driving to safety, in turn leaving the Newark police in the position of having to find a way to return the seventy-five Nazi sympathizers to their homes in safety.

Though clearly the melee was not instigated by the Friends, they nevertheless found themselves placed at a disadvantage with the law as a result of the confrontation. On May 23, Newark Director of Public Safety Michael P. Duffy sent orders to all precinct captains instructing them to prohibit further Friends meetings in their districts. Deputy Police Chief John F. Harris explained that the order was not meant to discriminate against pro-Nazi groups, claiming that the rule would apply to any meeting for which the possibility of trouble might exist.

Numerous other stories helped place American Nazi activities, including those of the Friends, in a negative light. Among other incidents, for example, wide press coverage was given to the actions of Nazi vandals in painting swastikas on Jewish synagogues. To a growing sector of the American public, becoming wary after seeing images of massive columns of Nazis marching in Germany, the Friends represented a hostile force whose presence in the United States needed to be checked.

In turn, the German government was forced to distance itself from the American pro-Nazi groups, and the negative publicity they were generating. German propaganda minister Joseph Goebbels assigned the German Consul General, Otto Kiep, the responsibility of hiring a public relations firm to distribute pro-German information leaflets, brochures, and booklets, though initially Kiep was only allotted $31,000 for this task. As Nazi authorities in Berlin grew more aware of, and alarmed at, the growing public furor in America over the activities of the Friends, they issued instructions to Spanknoebel to halt all inflammatory actions until further notice. The orders went unheeded.

Difficulties ensued for the Friends of New Germany, but by September 1 the group had nevertheless managed to pull together the resources and manpower to begin publishing their own journal, *Das neue Deutschland* [*The New Germany*]. The weekly publication was geared toward German legal resident aliens, as well as other sympathetic speakers of German; each issue also contained a special section, published in English to reach a wider audience, entitled the "German Outlook."

The U.S. Government Stepped In

Though some progress was made by the Nazi group with regard to public opinion, governmental interference was not long in coming. With memories of World War I still fresh in the minds of many Americans, with visual images of growing Nazi might in Germany being seen with increasing frequency, and as suspicions mounted about the possibilities of fifth-column activity in America, the American public began to speak with a considerably louder voice, calling for the policing of the Friends and other pro-Nazi organizations. To that end, on March 7, 1934, some 20,000 people came together at Madison Square Garden in New York, to observe a mock trial put on by the American Federation of Labor and the American Jewish Congress, entitled "Civilization vs. Hitler."

After Spanknoebel made known his connections to Nazi Germany, political leaders in Washington quickly developed their own suspicions regarding the Friends of New Germany. Among the rumors circulating in Washington was that Goebbels had personally ordered 300 propagandists to the United States, armed with millions of dollars, in an effort to influence public opinion throughout the country; such rumors, often untrue, themselves contributed to the creation of public hysteria against the German-American community. Consequently, in October 1933, the Chairman of the House Committee on Immigration and Naturalization, Samuel Dickstein, announced a forthcoming probe into the matter, with an arrest warrant to be issued for Spanknoebel. Before he could be served the warrant, Spanknoebel managed to escape the country, with assistance from other Nazi agents in the country.

Dickstein was not to be deterred. His committee, the Dickstein-McCormack Congressional Investigatory Committee, promptly made public its plans to investigate extensively the Friends of New Germany, beginning in April 1934. In January of the same year, Congress had voted, 168-31, to authorize the investigation of Nazi activities in America, overriding the objections of Congressman Terry Carpenter of Nebraska, who claimed that the investigations would only create racial prejudice. Meeting from April to July, the committee held relatively few public hearings; those that were open were conducted in an orderly fashion by McCormack, but the meetings presided over by Dickstein were often characterized by high levels of emotion, and even the taunting and baiting of witnesses. Worth noting is that the Committee invited not only Friends members and sympathizers, but also non-member German-Americans with no connection whatsoever to the group; the inevitable consequence for many of the outsiders was that their own loyalties, and those of the German-American community as a whole, unfairly began to be questioned. Members of the Friends present, however, did themselves, and other German-Americans, little service by accenting key moments in testimony with cries of "Heil Hitler!"

For its part, the general public followed the proceedings

with rapt attention, lending support to the committee through its growing obsession with the events which were unfolding. Many Americans turned on their radios and bought newspapers on a daily basis, in order to receive the latest news on the hearings. However, some members of the German-American community were considerably less enthused with the proceedings; in at least one case, the German language press dubbed the hearings the "Jewish Inquisition," and Dickstein America's number one "German hater," due to the harsh treatment of the German-American witnesses and the inclusion of non-Friends members in the hearings.

Berlin Curtailed Nazi Activity in America

Conscious that it was not in a position to fight the U.S. Government, Berlin quickly ordered German legal resident aliens in the United States to curtail all political activities. In October 1934, the head of the Steuben Society, Theodore Hoffman, was received in Berlin by Hitler; Hoffman expressed sharp criticism of the Friends, and pointed out that they were doing far more of a disservice than a service to German interests on both continents. The German government then announced that, henceforth, only German citizens would be allowed to become members of the American Nazi party, and that no Germans could be members of the Friends of New Germany as of October 1935, in an effort to allay American fears. The Friends of New Germany was given specific instruction to take on a more "American" image.

The sudden, unexpected departure of Spanknoebel and the Congressional investigation of the group left the Friends in a state of disarray. Once Kiep was recalled to Germany and the announced measures took effect, Nazi activity in the United States went through a period of reduced activity. For Nazism to survive or even prosper in

America, a transitional phase was in order, whereby the "Friends" organization could find new and more effective leadership, in a society renamed but virtually identical in its goals and policies.

The German announcements and actions, though, were largely ceremonial. The American Nazi movement was geared largely towards German legal resident aliens in the United States, not second- or third-generation German-Americans. While several other American "hate groups," such as the Ku Klux Klan, voiced their support for the Friends of New Germany and Nazi policy, few members actually involved themselves with the Nazi organization. The vast majority of the members of the Friends of New Germany were German legal resident aliens, for the most part recent immigrants from Germany. For that reason, the new German policy was destined to have only a minimal effect, offering little of use to the American Nazi sympathizers.

Realizing that, the House Committee continued its own investigations of the Friends of New Germany through much of 1934, and in February 1935 it finally came out with its report. For the most part, the report centered on the history of Nazi organizations in the United States, detailing their growth and development. While claiming that most German-Americans were loyal and honest people, but that there was sufficient evidence that Nazi activity within the United States had been on the rise in recent years, the committee took the opportunity to pat itself on the back for its work, stating that the adverse publicity the Nazi groups had received as a result of the hearings had served to halt their growth.

Friends Membership Continued to Rise

Such boasting, which sounded good in the media, was less than accurate in reality. From October 1934 to March 1935, membership in the Friends had doubled, and group activity was noticeably on the rise. Such activity was conducted in remarkably high-profile fashion, including expressing support for Bruno Hauptmann, the German-born carpenter accused of kidnapping and murdering Charles Lindbergh's baby; sponsoring a dance to celebrate Hitler's birthday; and conducting a mass rally in New York City.

Though Congressional action was something the Friends had little ability to manipulate, the group, to a certain degree, played upon German loyalties in traditional settlement areas, in an effort to strengthen its power base. By comparing itself with German National Socialism and reiterating the "Germanness" of the group, they were able to draw sympathy from many Germans; indeed, the Friends had a stated mission of making all German-Americans aware of their Germanness, in an effort to instill in German immigrants a sense of duty or obligation to the movement. Such a goal was achieved with relative ease in some areas, in which the German population tended to group together in well-defined communities, in clubs and societies which drew upon traditional German elements. The Friends liberally altered the basic components of National Socialism to suit the American audience they were trying to reach, adding anti-black overtones to their position against communism and the Jewish element.

Still, any successes the Friends may have had within the German community were more than negated by the reaction of the general American public. Seldom out of view due to their uniformed parading and rhetoric, the group found little acceptance or sympathy from even the most vocal First Amendment supporters in America. Increasing reports of persecution of Jews in Germany, and even attacks on Christian churches there, as well as a growing pattern of violence within Nazi circles, left most of the remaining open-minded observers with little cause or desire to support the Friends.

A German American Boy's Memories of Internment During World War II

Eberhard E. Fuhr

Eberhard E. Fuhr, a German immigrant, was seventeen when his father, mother, and younger brother were interned by the U.S. government in 1942, during World War II. Left to fend for themselves, Eberhard and his older brother were soon arrested and interned, too. In this first-hand account of his years spent in camps in Chicago; Crystal City, Texas; and Ellis Island, New York, Fuhr describes the anger, bewilderment, and frustration he felt due to his and his family's detainment. Upon his release in 1947, Fuhr completed his education, became a U.S. citizen, and worked many years for Shell Oil Company and Consoweld Corporation.

In August 1942, the U.S. government interned both my parents, German resident aliens. My 12-year-old brother was interned with them, even though he was an American citizen, having been born in Cincinnati. Had he not joined my parents, he would be sent to an orphanage, a fate shared by other internee children. My brother (18) and I (17) were allowed to stay home, but had to fend for ourselves. My brother soon left for an Ohio college where he had an athletic scholarship. I lived alone. I went back to Woodward High School in Cincinnati where we lived for my senior year. I was actively involved in student life. I lettered, belonged to student clubs and was even on the civil defense Bomb Squad.

Being Watched

I earned enough from my newspaper route to survive. Periodically, an FBI agent called to question me. Once they picked me up about 8 P.M., took me to their offices and questioned me for two hours under bright lights while toying with their guns. Their questions concerned family friends, attitudes about relatives in Germany and my parents' internment, what some neighbors (unnamed, of course) were saying about me, and the like. I clearly was being watched. In January 1943, my brother dropped out of college and went to work in a Cincinnati brewery.

On March 23, 1943, while in class at Woodward High School, two FBI agents arrested me. I was 17. When passing through the doorways, one would precede with a drawn pistol, while the other held my left arm. When we got outdoors, I was handcuffed. I never returned to school and did not graduate two short months later. I lost not only belongings in my school locker, but my dignity.

The FBI Agents then took me to my brother's place of employment where he was arrested. We were taken to the city police station where we were booked on suspicion, fingerprinted, and taken to the Hamilton County Prison. This was built in the mid-1800's and had a medieval look of turrets with very high walls. A 5-tiered cellblock dominated the interior. Each cell was about 5' × 10' with a metal bucket as a toilet, a bed hung from the wall by 2 chains, and walls about 2' thick. We were given prison clothes and locked into separate cells some distance apart.

Soon after the barred doors clanged shut, the prisoners, convicted criminals, began yelling vicious threats about Nazis, Krauts, Huns and what we could expect just as soon as the cells would open in the morning. We hardly slept. We were brought to the Federal Building for our hearings. No witnesses or counsel were permitted. While my brother had his hearing, I was given the *Cincinnati Enquirer*. In shock, I read: "Two brothers interned. They will have a hearing and they will be interned." We hadn't had our hearings yet, but the newspaper announced our arrest and internment.

Hearing Sealed Their Fate

After my brother, I had my hearing before the "Civilian Alien Hearing Board" to face the same people that interned my parents 7 months earlier. There were 5 or 6 members on the board. One question concerned a statement I supposedly made about Hitler when I was twelve. Another question concerned my attendance at Coney Island German American Day and German American picnics in 1939 and 1940. They even had glossy photos of me from the picnics. The high point was when they asked "What would you say to your German cousin if he came to you for sanctuary after coming up the Ohio River in his German U-boat." I said a sub couldn't come up the Ohio River, it only drafts 4 feet. Of course, they didn't like that response. Then they went into raw data, which is the "evidence" people call in and requires no substantiation because the informant is guaranteed anonymity. Any answers I gave seemed totally unacceptable, and I already knew that we were to be sent to Chicago for internment. I'd read it in the paper.

After questioning, my brother and I were again handcuffed and taken home. We were advised to take only enough clothes for about 2 days and to make sure all doors and windows were locked. This was the last time we ever saw the house. The contents were later looted: pictures,

stamp collection, violin, piano, furniture, keepsakes, irre-
placeable family memorabilia—all treasured by my mother
and gone forever. The house was lost to foreclosure. My parents could not afford to make the mortgage payments because they were interned. This was not unusual. Many
homes were lost during internment. The government was
not concerned about such matters. Incredibly, the elders of
our church even stopped by after my parents were interned
to demand their pledge. When we couldn't make payment,
my parents were dropped from the rolls of the church.

Treated as Criminals

We were taken back to the County prison and immediately
locked into our cells. The next morning, Federal Marshals
picked us for an auto trip to Chicago. This time we were
each handcuffed to a front ring in a belt buckled in the
belt. Additionally, we were handcuffed to each other, and,
when we stopped for the usual offices, one of the marshals
cuffed himself to one of us. These were needlessly intimate, embarrassing experiences. We were cuffed to a belt
and cuffed to each other, which required us to almost face
each other to move in any direction, never mind take care
of necessities.

We arrived late at night at 4800 South Ellis Avenue in
Chicago, but the other internees gave us a heartfelt welcome. We were there approximately three months. There
were about 20 inmates. This number stayed fairly consistent as internees were periodically sent to camps in North
Dakota and Texas, occasionally released, or newly interned.
Definitely no longer luxurious, the building was formerly
a small mansion complete with turrets, an 8' wrought iron
fence, and a garage that formerly was a stable.

Ten days after my arrival, I turned 18. I knew by law
that I was required to register for the draft and I was anx-
ious to do my duty. The internment facility director dis-

puted this. The Department of Justice advised him, however, not only that I had the right to register, but also that all males of 18, regardless of circumstances, were required to do so. Thus I registered at the Cook County Jail, which became my draft board during WWII.

Reunited with Family

In July 1943, we were sent to Crystal City, Texas, close to the Mexican border, on a heavily guarded train with about another 1,000 internees. The good news was that we were finally reunited with our parents and our younger brother. The bad news was that the fences were 12 feet high, with guard towers every 50 yards, and, except where irrigated, this was a harsh desert environment. Temperatures were often well over 100 degrees and the camp was filled with insects and scorpions. We received letters from friends and relatives, but these were heavily censored with much information cut out. Living conditions were tolerable at best.

In Crystal City I met Japanese for the very first time. The internee population was almost equally German and Japanese. Although the Japanese had their own cultural affairs, and events, we did compete in some sports. We generally had mutual access to all facilities. People came and went from the camp constantly, including Latin American Germans and Japanese who were brought from their countries primarily for exchange for American prisoners held by Axis countries. Many German and Japanese interned from America were also exchanged for American prisoners and suffered untold difficulties after the exchange. A marker commemorates only the internment of the Japanese at the camp. In general, the internment of German Americans is ignored, although at least 11,000 were interned, as well as a few thousand German Latin Americans.

After VE [Victory in Europe] Day, we thought we would be released, but after VJ [Victory in Japan] Day we were sure it would happen. It was not to be. President Harry Truman decided that those still interned at the end of the war were probably still "dangerous" and should be sent back to Germany. To my knowledge, this affected only the remaining several hundred persons of German ancestry still in custody. Everyone but internees of German descent left Crystal City by 1946. Those remaining, including my family, actually helped disassemble and close down the camp. Finally, in 1947, we were shipped to Ellis Island. The conditions were cramped, dirty and stultifying. I would never go back to Ellis Island. I spent too much time facing the back of the Statute of Liberty. I always felt that even though she had welcomed immigrants promising the American dream, she turned her back on us just because of our ancestry.

Starting Over

Finally, after a great deal of legal wrangling and a Congressional hearing, the Attorney General granted release to those remaining in custody in September 1947, two and a half years after the cessation of hostilities with Germany. My family had to start from scratch, burdened with the stigma of internment. For me, although not an even exchange, old friends were replaced with new friends. I met my wonderful wife, Barbara, in Crystal City. Lost time and opportunity was supplanted by an obsession not to waste either one. I completed high school and graduated from Ohio University with highest honors. After 12 years with Shell Oil, I earned an MBA from the University of Wisconsin, and held responsible jobs until retirement.

I was interned when I was 17 and released when I was 22. I did 4½ years of time for being German. Without experiencing internment, no one can appreciate the intense terror of government power and the despair of hopelessness and endless time one feels. In addition, an internee must suffer humiliation, stigmatization, and suspect "friends" who may have given damning "evidence" to the FBI, like whether one said something about Hitler at age 12. Understandably, many bear the psychological scars throughout their lives. Many have gone to their graves never speaking of their internment to their families, my brother included. A large majority of internees still do not speak out. We in the German American community must support and encourage these people to tell their stories at last without fear of recrimination. They are not criminals, but persons caught in a web of wartime hysteria. German Americans must support their people like the Japanese and Italian Americans before them.

A government has the right and duty to protect itself. But in America, civil liberties should not be cast aside so freely, even in times of war. Frequently, as a result of rumor and innuendo, families were torn apart and homes lost. Those who were a real threat to the U.S. could have been controlled by means which did not violate civil liberties so severely. No internee was ever convicted of a crime. Spies and saboteurs were not interned. They were executed after receiving due process, the same due process internees, who were here legally, never received. The tragedy of Japanese American relocation is well known primarily because of the tremendous effort of their people. Are our people less deserving of recognition? German Americans and our organizations must insist that our government finally acknowledge the wrongs committed against our people because of our ethnicity. No one will do it for us. Likewise, we remaining internees, much as we would like to keep these experiences locked away in a dark corner, owe it to others to publicize the whole story so that what we suffered never happens again.

A Family Exiled from Nazi Germany Adjusts to a New Life

Hertha Nathorff

Hertha Nathorff and her husband were Jewish physicians in Berlin when they were forced to flee Nazi Germany because of Adolf Hitler's plan to eradicate Jews. Nathorff and her family were among the approximately 130,000 German Jews who sought refuge in America between 1933 and 1945. In this excerpt from Nathorff's diary, she describes her and her family's arrival in New York in 1940 and how they found life in America to be much different from what they had known in Germany. Nathorff had to take a succession of menial jobs to support her family while her husband studied to pass the American medical exams. Although Nathorff dreamed of regaining her own status as a physician, she came to realize that the obstacles were too great. Nevertheless, she eventually was able to establish a career in public health as a nurse and teacher of home-healthcare workers.

February 22, 1940

After exchanging greetings and embraces, which hardly improved my sense of vertigo, after much deliberation about what to do with our luggage (we had brought some gifts for friends from their children in England, which we gave to them right away), we looked about, somewhat

Hertha Nathorff, "Arriving in New York," *Hitler's Exiles: Personal Stories of the Flight from Nazi Germany to America*, edited by Mark M. Anderson. New York: The New Press, 1998. Copyright © 1998 by Mark M. Anderson. All rights reserved. Reproduced by permission of The New Press. (800) 233-4830.

dejected, and then someone asked: "So where are you planning to stay?" No one had thought of reserving even a simple hotel room for us, no one had thought of our accommodations—probably for fear of being left with the bill! I couldn't believe my eyes. I saw my husband grow pale, and he looked out at the ocean, at the ship by the dock, to the horizon, thinking that we once had a homeland, a house, a place of our own.

My friend Friedel whispered to me: "If I'd even dreamed that your relatives wouldn't take care of a room, I would have reserved one for you." My cousin must have heard her. She had been like a sister to me, and during her student years in Berlin our home and our heart were always open to her. "*Well,*" she said suddenly, "my husband won't be home this weekend, so you and your boy can stay with me until then." In the meantime my husband's childhood friend offered to put my husband up. We had to accept because we didn't have the money for even a few nights in a hotel. This way we were "safe" for at least two days and nights. After that, I thought to myself, I'll be sure to find some job so that we can afford a furnished room. Thus our new country divided us in the very first hours after our arrival—what a sad omen. With great effort we shrugged off our disappointment. We'll soon be back together, whispered my husband to me as we left each other. But I could read in his eyes the sadness of his heart, just as he sensed my sorrow. I remained silent and mechanically let everything wash over me, but I know that my heart, once so quick to forgive and forget, will always start bleeding again when I hear the question: "So where are you planning to stay?"

February 25, 1940

The two days and nights with my cousin were dreary and full of torment. For the first time in my life I have felt what it means to be "tolerated." My food remained stuck in my throat, because my stomach was deprived of food and drink during our famished period in England and then on the boat. Now I have to learn how to eat again.

Thanks to an acquaintance we happened to run into, we have found accommodations in a "Shelter for the Homeless." A rabbi, Stephen Wise, originally from Europe, has opened a house for destitute immigrants. The Congress House on 68th Street, near Central Park, will be our home for the next three to four weeks—for you can stay that long until you have found work and lodgings. We sleep in narrow dormitories, men and women separated, we take our meals in the canteen at small, nicely set tables, we frequent people from our own cultural circle. So many of our acquaintances are here, even an aunt with her daughter and son-in-law. Why didn't anyone think of sending us here right from the start? We would have been spared so much humiliation.

Today we took our first Sunday walk in New York, here in the nearby Central Park. How beautiful the park is: snow is everywhere, and it falls like powdered silver from the trees with their gleaming, icy pinecones. It is bitter cold and the people we meet have red, friendly, laughing faces. Joyful, laughing people—how long have we not seen such a sight! Like children in a fairytale, we march through the snow-covered ballroom with its column-like trees, searching for our way and using the skyscrapers to point us in the right direction. How fascinating this city is, how immense, how beautiful.

Will the city give us work and food? Early tomorrow morning I will start looking. I want to earn a new homeland for myself.

February 27, 1940

The hoop-jumping has begun again, by which I mean the trips I have to make to various organizations in order to get advice and assistance for our new life and, above all, to find work. For that is one thing I am sure of: I don't want to live off "charity"—I don't, my husband doesn't, not even my child. We stand in a long line, waiting until we finally can talk to someone and make our plight clear. Clear? But how? I myself, who studied in a high school where ancient languages were taught, never learned English. And how far does my husband's knowledge of the language go? We'll find out. These counselors are partly true-born Americans who speak only English, partly emigrants who arrived a few years earlier than us, encountered fewer difficulties, and act as if they don't understand a word of German. Our situation is desperate. Our sponsor died shortly before our arrival. His will, no doubt very complicated, will take years to be settled. Much was left unclear. From the beginning his heirs, clearly interested in receiving their father's fortune—worth millions—while honoring his obligations, have been trying to keep the latter as small as possible and, understandably enough, to incur no new ones.

On top of that, in a personal meeting with him in Germany years ago, I once said I would never be a burden to him. At that time I still believed that, if we indeed had to emigrate, I would be able to bring a major portion of our savings and our belongings with us. How wrong I was. We arrived completely destitute. And the hope that we would at least get the container with all our belongings out of hock—furniture, household items, dishes, linen, clothing, pictures, carpets, precious collections of porcelain and glass, and last but not least two complete sets of medical tools—now appears illusory despite all my efforts to obtain a loan for the seventy-two dollars we still owe.

When I finally made this clear to the social worker, she said to me: "Furniture, housewares—what's the point? You're too attached to your fancy lifestyle and elegant apartment in Germany! You don't need them here. You want to be a doctor again? Get that crazy idea out of your head. We have enough doctors here, we don't want any more, and especially not any lady doctors. Your husband and you should take a job as domestic housekeepers. That way you'll have a roof over your heads, some food in your stomachs, and on top of it you'll have a salary and can start saving."

So this is the kind of assistance we could expect. Dumbfounded, I remained silent in the face of so little understanding and sympathy. Then I said, stuttering: "Fine, we'll take a job in someone's home as housekeepers. But only I will work, I can work enough for two; my husband has to study so he can get his doctor's license. Who knows, despite all the doctors you have here, maybe one day you'll be pleased to have me as a doctor as well."

I asked her to give me the name of an appropriate family, and tomorrow I'll start working.

March 7, 1940

I haven't written in my diary for a while, but have been gathering new "experiences." The other emigrant women and I all agree on one thing: if we had ever treated our servants in this way, they never would have been so faithful to us for years and even decades. I sometimes smile at the thought of what my dear servant Minna would say if she could see me now. How often she pushed me out of the kitchen saying, "This is no kind of work for you," whenever I tried to lend a hand. Today, no job is too heavy or too dirty for me. People often call me "dirty refugee," words I understand perfectly well. I work, I work for the modest daily bread we need. What pains me most is to have to stay away from home, even overnight, when in addition to the normal housework I have to take care of an old, sick woman, who calls me a dozen times a night, often just to bother me because she can't fall asleep.

Today I applied for a new position. When the "lady of the house" saw me, she could only utter the words "lousy

Nazi spy" and slammed the door in my face. What should I answer when confronted with such small-minded prejudice?

March 11, 1940

Today I'm at home again. The baby I was taking care of, in addition to watching over four other children and doing all the housework, doesn't need me anymore. I start my next job the day after tomorrow. How wonderful it is to be free again, to be able to rest, although it won't be much of a rest. Our room needs sweeping, the laundry has to be done, I also have to shop and sew—and I'd also like to study some English in my spare time!

My son goes to school far away from here. He earns his bus fare and whatever else he needs by delivering packages after school. The poor boy—he's so quiet now, and recently he came home blue from the cold.

Silently, doggedly, my husband studies for the English exam he must pass in order to be admitted to the medical board exam. He works without ever letting a complaint cross his lips. But his eyes look serious and sad, and the lovely sparkle that greets me when I come home disappears quickly.

Our home: a miserable room I rented because I mistook the fire escape with the burglar bars for a balcony. One bed for the two of us, as narrow as the one in Berlin that each of us had, so roomy and comfortable. Our son sleeps on a small cot in a windowless alcove. The so-called kitchen is, as is typical here, a small room which they call a kitchenette. The bathroom, no matter how bad it looks, is ours alone. And when we close the door, this is our home, not a furnished room in someone else's apartment where we would constantly be with other people.

We only have two chairs, and they wobble, but I don't care. I'm hardly ever "at home," and so father and son can at least both sit at the small table for the "sumptuous" meals they prepare for themselves. With a few throw rugs from our suitcase I've tried to give the room a homey look. It's not much help. The smell of poverty which greets you as you climb the narrow stairwell fills the entire house. We don't have visitors—who could climb such stairs, who would visit such poor relatives or colleagues? Oh, I'm so ashamed, not for myself but for the others who let us live in such circumstances and won't loan us the few dollars it would take to rent a decent apartment. This room costs us eight dollars a week, which is much more than it's worth. (Why shouldn't the people here also profit from the misfortune of others?) But I earn only ten to fifteen dollars a week, from which I must pay for transportation, small shoe repairs, etc. Only then can we think of food and drink— on average we have one dollar per day to spend. Nowadays I often say "I've already eaten at work," and skip a meal. One can still train one's stomach.

April 2, 1940

From one job to the next. How hectic life is in this country. There's not even enough time to admire all the beautiful things in this fascinating city. The technology, the tall buildings, the bridges, tunnels, subway—I'm constantly amazed, but where is the time to take it all in? To go to a museum or, a special treat, to a movie or a concert—who has the time and the money?

My husband is more taciturn than ever. I sense how humiliated he feels because he has to live off my salary. I console him, saying he will soon be back in his old profession and then I'll have an easy life and will always be able to stay with him and our son, and can even study as well. What would he say if he knew that I secretly take his notes and attempt to study during the night when I can't fall asleep?

Today I received the first letter from my parents. They try to appear confident, to calm our worries about them in the old country, to encourage us not to give up. Dear, good parents, if only you knew . . . I'm going back to work. This time night duty—and I cry bitter, bitter tears. My husband mustn't see my tears. He is so peculiar, and I sense a glass wall between us—no, no, that mustn't be.

April 6, 1940

My mother has passed away. The news hits me hard. My poor father, now he's all alone. My son tries to console me, and asks me not to go to work today. How could I? We'd have less to eat then, and mother wouldn't have approved of that. She was a woman who lived only for others and put her own life last. I intend to be a daughter worthy of her dear mother. I'll go to work and bear my pain alone—even my husband can't understand me anymore. Where are we heading to?

May 10, 1940

The days pass in a constant flurry of work. How demeaning it is. Not the work in itself—I don't mind what I have to do to meet our modest living expenses. But the way one is treated. Impudent men who dare to put their arm around you—I can put up with them. But these women who want to be "ladies"—they are saucy, inconsiderate, with no sense of tact. Many of them look at you as if you were an animal or less than that—who knows?—and they have no understanding of our fate. How could they? What is happening over there—war, murder, immorality—is so far away, but I fear that even this "far away" will someday be quite close. I myself have no more confidence, no hope that things will ever be different. Hitler has now invaded Holland. I had predicted this and people laughed at me for such crazy ideas. All my hope is gone now. I pleaded with them, "Help us before it's too late, save my profession which means my life to me." Now they want to loan us the pitiful sum we needed to get our belongings sent over from Holland. Now, when it's too late. Everything is lost, I can tell, I'll never become a doctor again, and yet I want to fight for it even though I'm again without a job for the moment. I think I take care of people too well and work too hard; then they don't need me anymore. Besides, the people I'm sent to are not well off; otherwise they wouldn't ask for help from an immigrant organization, help that is cheap and hardworking, people they can count on. . . .

June 5, 1940

My husband has passed his language exam. I'm happy, but nonetheless, I can't keep up with him the way I used to. I have to go to work while he's been preparing for the exam with his colleagues.

It's my birthday today. My husband and son have tried to make me happy with a few small presents. I put on a good face—love can also sometimes pretend. We get little mail from Germany. I'm exhausted from worrying about our relatives and friends, as well as about our own lives. Day and night I think about what's going on over there, and here at night when the trolley rattles through the street I wake up from a half-sleep and think about the bombings we lived through in England. What's happening to the people over there? Are they still alive?

Our social circle here is composed almost entirely of immigrants, almost all of them people we knew earlier and who represent a piece of our homeland as we do to them. Many of us are of "mixed" marriage, as the nice Nazi term would have it—German women who emigrated with their Jewish husbands and who now, like me, support their husbands, work for them until they can get back into their profession or find another job. It takes a long time, very long. And the German husbands with their Jewish wives—they emigrated with and for their wives rather than divorce them and stay in Germany to serve their country. We remain faithful friends and try to give each other support. But the uncried tears can be heard in our voices when we speak about the old country.

I myself have just had some luck. I start tomorrow as a night nurse in a hospital. How will this job turn out? In any case, how thankful I am to my old and famous professor, who, as long as I was his assistant, had me do so many jobs that were not, strictly speaking, a doctor's business. A woman must do everything, he said—he who actually was opposed to women doctors. And now this woman really does everything she is asked to.

My husband shakes his head and remains silent. Does he sense all my heart's sufferings, does he realize that wherever I go, men are courting me? In vain, because my heart belongs to him, even when it is sad and discouraged.

June 14, 1940

"Bronx Express"—that was the name of a play that was all the rage in Berlin. Only now do I know what the Bronx Express really is, because I take it everyday to work. The train whizzes from Manhattan to the Bronx. I commute evenings with a Swiss woman who is actually an actress; for the time being we are both night nurses in a hospital. It's hard work, and I don't have an easy time of it because I do lots of things that the others refuse to do. "You make it harder for us when you run to the patients at the first ring of the bell," one of the nurses tells me. Someone else yells at me because I rub down the patients on hot summer nights with a mixture of alcohol and water. And a doctor put me in my place for having dared to call him because of a child with appendicitis.

"How dare you make a diagnosis? I'm in charge of diagnoses," he hissed at me.

I stuttered a bit, then said: "I promise not to do it again, but the child doesn't have pneumonia as the charts say, it's a typical case of appendicitis."

"Get the kid ready for an operation and bring him into the operating room."

Of course I rushed to get the child to the operating room and wanted to go in and watch the operation. Again he put me in my place:

"Go back to your station. You'll be called when the operation is over and you can bring the child back. An operating room isn't for you. You wouldn't be able to stand it."

He's probably right—I wouldn't be able to stand it to have to watch someone else operate. I run away, my tears start flowing; just get away from here, don't think, do your job without thinking. How long has it been that I stood at the operating table myself? Just don't think about it. What's more, there's a doctor who shows up every night no matter where I am, and today he started a conversation. He's looking for a nurse for his office—would I be interested?

"Can I ask my husband what he thinks?"

I laugh, laugh up there on the roof garden where the night staff is allowed to go and rest during breaks. How beautiful these nights are, and the view from the tall building onto the shimmering lights of the city—it's almost a fairy tale. But down there, a few stories below, is work, sickness, suffering and pain. Here too.

[Hertha Nathorff takes several other jobs, including one with her child in a summer camp in the Catskills while her husband remains in New York.]

December 20, 1940

My husband has passed his [medical] exam—the whole thing, on the very first try. No one can believe it, and I myself have trouble grasping it. The exam is over, he's a doctor again, soon he'll have a praxis. I start dreaming, perhaps one day I too . . . No, I can't even write it down. I know only that now I will work even harder to earn some money, for we have nothing in our apartment, nothing with which to set up a new life. But we're going to make it, and there are only four more days until Christmas. I'll have the day off, my employers promised me they would get a replacement, how nice. I can't speak or write, I can only fold my hands in silence, happy that fate has proved so merciful to us after all.

December 25, 1940

Christmas. Yesterday evening a German-American acquaintance, one of the few we've made over here until now, brought us a wreath with lights. And so a light shines on us again after all the dark days. We sat quietly and peacefully at home, all three of us on the narrow bed, pressed close together as we tried to sing the old Christmas carols. Our thoughts strayed far and wide, back to our homeland. The unfortunate people we love and worry about, where might they be now? Are they too thinking about us? Yes, I can feel it, for there is a faithfulness which knows no dividing barriers or walls or oceans.

Christmas, peace on earth—where?

None of us wants to speak about our life back there. We know how much it would hurt, and today is Christmas, a holiday. We took a walk through Central Park. It is glorious in its winter splendor, and all the happy, laughing people on our way made my heart lighter. Perhaps one day we too will stroll through Central Park happy and laughing, sit quietly on a bench late in the evening and enjoy the sea of lights, the blinking lights of the skyscrapers all around us, and our hearts won't cringe in pain as they did today.

A Holocaust Survivor Comes to America

Dorothy Rabinowitz

Beginning in 1945 at the culmination of World War II, 250,000 German Jewish survivors of the Holocaust immigrated to the United States. Their reasons for leaving Germany were varied: Some could no longer envision a life in their homeland while others believed their lives would be in danger if they stayed in Germany. In this selection Dorothy Rabinowitz describes the journey of Emil Wolf (a pseudonym), who lost his entire family during the Holocaust and came to America in 1946 after being liberated from a concentration camp. The author tells how Wolf slowly began adjusting to his new life, only to be dealt a crushing blow when he learned he would have to be confined for treatment of tuberculosis. The author is a *Wall Street Journal* editorialist who won the Pulitzer Prize in 2001 for Distinguished Commentary. She is the author of *About the Holocaust: What We Know and How We Know It* and *New Lives: Survivors of the Holocaust Living in America*, the source of this selection.

In 1946, the *SS Marine Flasher* carried among its passengers to America a stern-looking young man named Emil Wolf, who, in his mid-twenties, appeared to be ten years older. This impression was due to the heavy horn-rimmed glasses he wore, and also to his eyes, which peered out gravely and judgmentally at all that they beheld. At the time of his arrival, he already knew English quite well; he had been born into comfortable circumstances, of a sort that had provided him, before the war, with an English tutor, in addition to the Greek, Latin, and French lessons that were the standard educational fare for the child of a cultured German family. His parents, Berlin Jews, had had two sons close together in age, and on both of them they had lavished a loving and intense ambition that they should rise in the world. It was intended by their father, a successful merchant, that his sons should study law, but this ambition, like all plans and thoughts about the future, became lost in the events that overtook them in Germany.

Arriving in New York

Of the family, the older son had survived, a lanky white-skinned figure who carried a battered suitcase under one arm when he arrived at the Port of New York. It must at moments have been obvious that he was young, despite the aged judgment written on his face, at least it was to the Port of New York customs guard who had singled him out for attention. When the guard pointed at the old suitcase and asked him what he had inside of it, he told the man that there were just some old clothes in it.

"Take that bag and that junk, son," the guard told him, smiling, "and throw it into the river there. You won't need it; America's gonna be good to you, you'll see." Sensibly tightening his hold on the suitcase, which contained his other suit and several shirts, he stared at the guard. Then, overcome by the unexpected kindness of this greeting, he did not know what to say in return; in the end, he simply thanked the guard and proceeded on the hot July day to find his way uptown.

The social worker in the agency office called the number of an uncle who lived in New York. The uncle was elderly, a first cousin to Emil Wolf's father, and a prosperous man who had escaped Germany and come to America in 1938. After identifying herself, the social worker told the uncle happily that a member of his family had come out of Germany alive.

"*Alle tot*," the uncle barked at her.

"No, they are not all dead," the social worker told him.

"I tell you they are dead. *Alle tot*," the man said fiercely.

"What would you say," the social worker persisted, "if I told you that Emil Wolf is alive and standing here in my office?" After grunting again that everyone was dead, the uncle said he would come and see for himself who was standing in her office. The object of this conversation was not destined to stop long in the home of his uncle, who recognized him and took him home with him, if not, as was amply clear, with great happiness. His aunt cried over him, and the fate of the family, but clearly the couple would have been happier without this emissary from the world of the dead, come to upset their patched-together lives. They wanted to think no more about the dark experiences they had known themselves in Germany, or the far darker imaginings they had of the things that occurred to those who had stayed when they had left. They were neither indifferent nor cruel people; merely ones who wished no more interruptions in the ongoing tide of their lives, people who had been cowed by upheaval, so that for comfort now they had always to clutch to themselves the familiar routine of their days, to hold with a tight fist to all that they had.

Moving to the South

Emil Wolf passed the first week staring absorbedly at every sight he saw in Manhattan, which impressed him and which was precisely as he had imagined it would be from his reading. At the end of it, however, he decided that he would have to join relatives in the South who were expecting him—the ones who had signed the affidavit that brought him to America. Furthermore, the long lugubrious conversations with his aunt made him intensely uncomfortable. The two of them sat together in the living room of the large upper West Side apartment, with its enormous dining table the aunt and uncle had brought with them from Germany, its silver pieces, urns, trays, and candelabrum that shone brightly from the glass cabinets and tables, in glaring relief to the heavy dark furnishings.

After the first day, what passed between him and his aunt were not conversations, actually. The old woman would sigh and repeat the names of the dead relatives. Then a silence would come, followed by tears. Invariably, with the room thus filled with the sound of his aunt's crying, Emil Wolf felt restless and guilty; he had, he knew, brought these tears on the household by his presence in it.

The Memphis relatives were generous, kindly people inclined to worry much over him, and as poor as the New York relatives were rich. His aunt, a soft-eyed nervous woman, insisted that he needed rest, only rest; his uncle agreed. So far as his plans were concerned, an agency social worker in Memphis advised him that he could get a job and go to night school if he wanted. It was at the meetings with the social workers and the psychiatric counselors, whom the social agencies employed to deal with the immigrants, that a resentment began to grow in him. Neither their psychological queries nor the answers he gave produced anything useful for him; he loathed the probing, personal questions, and the superior air of the questioners, though he contained his loathing behind an iron stare. As far as he was concerned, they were not, these fat women and these officious men, entitled to hear everything they wanted to know about him, to treat him as though, beyond question, they were his superiors.

They did not look like his superiors. One squinted at

him, and looked pleased with herself, as though she were doing him a great kindness, when she told him to take a chair. There was another, a man, who took notes and asked him questions such as whether he felt guilty.

"Guilty about what?" Emil Wolf asked the man, who looked thoughtfully at him.

"Guilty about surviving?" the man suggested. Emil Wolf regarded the man in silence for a time, and then shook his head no. The man, who was a psychiatric social worker of some kind, nodded acceptingly and wrote his answer down.

"I mean guilt about survival; you don't feel upset from time to time that other people in your family died and that you lived? That's what the question means," the worker explained in an encouraging manner. "Now, do you feel guilty about this sometimes?"

Exactly what answer he gave the worker, he could not later remember, except that it was a truthful one: that the thought of feeling guilty for being alive had never entered his mind.

Driven to Be Independent

The questions and the interviews produced only a bad temper and no practical proposals. A week after he arrived in Memphis, he wandered downtown alone and, over the protests of his aunt, got himself a job as a shoe salesman. He had given up the idea of going to school, and was driven now by an urge to be independent as quickly as possible. The Memphis relatives were poor, and in need themselves; he could not be dependent on them for money. He wanted to be dependent on no one: that was his obsession. His evenings, which he had at first spent in his room engaged in his old pursuits—reading the novels of his favorites, Mann, Conrad, and Dostoevsky, and listening to music—he now began to spend going about Memphis, sometimes to the movies, but more often wandering, look-ing at the shopwindows. The work at the shoe store was not hard, but the hours he put in were long, and he was glad of it, glad of the eighty-five dollars a week that he took home and that—partly, at least—put him beyond the reach of charitable organizations and their questions. Other people, of course, asked questions of him not very different from those the psychiatric social workers asked. He was not of-fended by these, particularly since they were not asked by agency workers, people he felt constrained to answer be-cause they had authority. No refugee found it easy to dis-miss the fact that agency workers were officials, and they might yet have the power to send him where he did not wish to go or to withhold what he wanted to receive.

Often survivors who arrived in America were asked, "Why did you survive?" The question meant, actually, "Why did you survive and not the others?" The implica-tion, which was not subtle, was the result of stories Amer-icans had heard of the tooth-and-nail fight for survival in the death camps, and of the efficiency of the Nazi death machine. As the facts about the concentration camps were revealed after the war, it became reasonable to conclude that amoral behavior was a technique of survival. From this conclusion there took hold, as a sort of common wis-dom, the more simplistic idea that the only people who could have survived were those who would perform the amoral acts necessary to preserve life in the circumstances the Nazis created: those who could steal the bread from other starved men, those who could gain favor by report-ing someone else or by performing other, more unspeak-able deeds. In one of the more noteworthy manifestations of obedience to the common wisdom, there were survivors themselves, many years after the war, who had learned to say that it was true: "The best died; the worst of us lived." Invariably, such observations were uttered with that air of self-approval which always betrays the presence of an orthodoxy; and while there were doubtless many who believed in the truth of these remarks because of what they had themselves seen during the war, it is likely that as great a number believed it because of the things they had heard after the war—or, more precisely, they chose to believe that they believed it.

Incomprehensible Questions

In the years just after the war, however, the survivors were not at all prepared for the questions that were asked of them, nor were they familiar with the idea of a survivor image, much less obedient to one—as, many years later, some of them became.

One learned that it was quite possible he would be asked, straightforwardly or otherwise, by what means he had purchased his life; and often those who were asked these questions learned that such questioning was a pattern, best to be stored away with other strange responses they had encountered, each new one a proof to them that they and their experiences were utterly incomprehensible to all those who had not been part of it. They soon learned that they might be asked, by friends and relatives, what it was like to starve, and after being told that starvation was very bad, the friends and relatives might respond that yes, they knew, because there had also been shortages of many things in America during the war, such as sugar. The survivors learned that they might be told to tell the truth: surely once they must have been given a dessert after the main meal in all the time they were in the concentration camp? Never even a piece of cake? There were also those whose friends and relatives were intent on hearing nothing, and asked no questions whatever, out of a kind wish not to bring up unhappy memories. This was a generous attitude, but one that also served to isolate those survivors who could not successfully pretend that they had been nowhere, and that nothing of significance had happened to them in the five years or more that they had spent in captivity or hiding.

Blending In

Emil Wolf's Southern Jewish society inclined to the last attitude, which was according to his wishes and not in the least disturbing to him, for more and more he wished not to stand out in that society but to melt into it. Almost to his own surprise, he found himself enjoying life in Memphis, and there were good reasons for it. After the day's work at the shoe store, he hurried home, now not to sit in his room and read, but to ride around the city with one or another of his friends, people his aunt had introduced him to, and particularly the girls, who were all of good families. As the aunt pointed out to him, the effect of these girls on him was tongue-loosening. One in particular, a tall brown-haired girl, listened to every sentence he uttered as though this were the last chance that would be granted her to hear anything of interest to her in life. The result was that the number of sentences he uttered was greatly increased. Evening after evening, he took leave of his aunt and uncle and jumped into the car in which his friends waited for him. With them, he would hold forth on whatever it was that interested them at a given time: movies, music, or simply small talk. He never spoke of the war, or his experiences, and no one asked him about those things.

At the end of a year in Memphis, he seemed at his ease. Though the stern judgmental expression of his eyes remained, other things in his appearance had changed; for example, he had begun to smile often and quickly, a thing that had come naturally to him in the company of his Memphis friends, all of whom were cheerful people, who smiled a great deal themselves; in fact, they smiled most of the time, in company. His aunt and uncle were happy that their relative no longer sat by himself in the evenings, although his aunt was sometimes uneasy at the way he rushed out of the house after a day's work, and at the late hours he kept; she had never got over the idea that he needed rest.

Then, at the end of a year and a half, he became informally engaged to the tall brown-haired girl who listened with such devotion to everything he said. The girl was from a wealthy Jewish family in Memphis from whom the young couple could probably expect financial help, but even had she not been, people had married on far less than the eighty-five dollars a week he made at the shoe store. From time to time, he still thought of going to school as soon as he had made the money to do it. At work, surrounded by shoeboxes, he could sometimes catch a glimpse of himself in the store mirror as he emerged from the clutter, shoe in hand, ready to fit it on a customer's outstretched foot. At such moments he wondered how his parents would feel if they had lived, seeing him this way, on his knees, selling shoes: how unimaginable it would have been to them, at one time.

A Setback

Usually, though, at work he would turn all his attention to making sales, at which he was very good. Indeed, he made more than any other salesman in the store, and when he fell ill with a bad cold and a cough that did not go away, his employers and his relatives blamed it on his zest for work. But the cough remained. One of the salesmen told him that he should go and have an X-ray, advice that he one day obeyed, with the result that he found himself having to go back to one of the hated social agencies to seek help in getting admitted to a hospital for the treatment of tuberculosis. The center for treatment in America was the Denver

Jewish hospital, to which he was sent. He was, as it turned out, one of a good number of people whose health broke down a few years or more after the liberation, the result of damage done during the years in the camps or in hiding. Tuberculosis cases were common among the survivors, in some of whom the symptoms of the disease did not become evident until long after the war.

Miserably, he listened to the instructions of the agency social worker who had arranged his transportation and his admission to the hospital. The agency treated him well, even generously, in his illness, a fact that was not lost upon him. Later, he explained to himself that it was not when one was down and out that one had to worry about the social workers, but when one was up and independent.

Old Fears Return

He was worse than down and out when he left Memphis. For one thing, his girl had broken their engagement shortly after he told her the reasons for his trip to Denver. In addition, the prospect of leaving Memphis for a new and unknown place, and one moreover where he would be confined again, filled him with a depression more terrible than anything he had known since the war. It was worse, in some ways, than anything he had ever known, for the new beginnings he had made in Memphis, the friends, the girl, the independence he had worked so hard for—all had been swept away overnight.

In Pleasantville, Missouri, he had to change trains. All the way to Missouri, his depression had grown deeper; he thought of being locked up in a hospital, of the possibility of never being released, of being told to leave America. There was no energy in him to think of brighter possibilities; simply, the thought of new beginnings, whether it was the life in the hospital or the one he would have to take up if he recovered, was impossible to bear. On the platform

where he waited, he saw the Colorado Eagle roaring toward
the station. Just as the Eagle sped in, he moved to the edge
of the platform and leaned far over it. He stood that way
for only a moment before the engineer pulled the brakes,
sending sparks high in the air, and brought the train to a
sudden halt quite close to him. On the Eagle, he opened a
bottle of whiskey he had put in his suitcase, and he began
to drink. He drank all night, almost as much in one night
and morning as he might put away in two years, so that by
the time he was close to arriving in Denver, he was, as he
had planned to be, very drunk. Stupefied and sick as he
was, he nevertheless noticed the mountains outside of Denver blazing at him from the train windows. The sight was
not a comfort, for it intruded itself on his depression.
When the train came to a stop, he staggered off into the
white Denver sunlight, where he was found soon enough
and packed into a station wagon. The hospital driver, also a
former patient, had a number tattooed on his forearm.

"Give it a chance," the man told him, and said no more.
The silence between them was effortless. Looking green-
ish, and feeling worse than he looked, Emil Wolf closed
his eyes and leaned back in the seat, every now and then
opening them a bit to look out the window, thinking that
he was now very far from Memphis, that he was now like
his old friend Hans Castorp, going up into the mountains
from which he might not return.

Being German American in Modern Times

La Vern J. Rippley

After nearly four hundred years of German immigration to
the United States, it is reasonable to wonder if immigrants
and their descendants still have a sense of their German
identity and heritage. In the following selection author La
Vern J. Rippley explains that ethnic pride still exists among
many German Americans, but it has been greatly diluted
with the passage of time. Rippley notes that as recently as
the 1950s, German Americans were actively pursued as a
group for their vote. The author concludes, however, that
although many German publications and organizations are
still active today, most German Americans have become
thoroughly assimilated into American life. Rippley, chair
of the German Department at St. Olaf College, Northfield,
Minnesota, is the author of several books about German
immigration, including *The German-Americans*, the
source of this selection.

For several years after World War II, Americans of German
descent found it a handicap to admit to a German back-
ground, although it was not due to anti-German hostility the
way it was during World War I. Ethnic pride in being German was gone. New immigrants from Germany and from
the German-speaking areas of Eastern Europe were welcomed in America but they arrived with a mark of Cain—

La Vern J. Rippley, *The German-Americans.* Boston: Twayne Publishers, 1976. Copyright © 1976 by G.K. Hall & Co. All rights reserved. Reproduced by permission of The
Gale Group.

the designation "displaced person." The DP was treated fairly, but he was a third-class citizen, not much better off than the blacks and other minorities. Quickly, the DP perceived that acceptance was hindered rather than helped by joining whatever vestiges were left of *Deutschtum* [Germanness] in the United States. Success was to be found in abandoning the immigrant image to join the mainstream of American professional and labor careers at the earliest possible opportunity. At any rate, the new immigrants did not identify with the romantic, nostalgic Old World culture which was characteristic of the older German-Americans.

Courting the German-American Vote

American politicians, however, were not so quick in abandoning their faith in ethnic politics as they prepared for elections in the early 1950s. Having learned their lesson in 1948, the Republicans formulated strategy for 1952. A chief salient of their organization was the Ethnic Origins Division of the Republican National Committee. By June, 1952, the committee had made available detailed studies of the distribution of Americans of foreign origin, broken down by politically strategic states, cities, and Congressional districts. It also gathered data on foreign-language publications, ethnic churches, and organizations, and cut phonograph records in the respective foreign languages. Each edition featured a political talk tract, the *Star-Spangled Banner*, and the national anthem of the country of origin. The plan worked successfully on German-Americans, in part because in Dwight Eisenhower they recognized one of their own descendants, if only faintly. Eisenhower was, however, not entirely without liabilities among German voters, some of whom felt that he was at least partly responsible for the Carthaginian peace that had been imposed upon Germany. Some also charged that Eisenhower had to share responsibility for the half-implemented Morgenthau Plan, which aimed at reducing the industrial might of the Fatherland to zero. Inevitably, critics also saddled the general with the heartless exiling of some 200,000 German prisoners of war who were turned over to Russia for slave labor after the conclusion of hostilities. The plan, known as "Operation Keelhaul," was particularly harsh toward the Russian-Germans, for they were Soviet citizens who had fled from their native land and joined the German Army as a means to escape communism.

As the 1952 campaign went into its home stretch, the Democrats sensed that they had neglected to concentrate enough energy on the ethnic vote. On the stump for Adlai E. Stevenson, [Harry] Truman complained bitterly that the Republicans were playing a game of gutter politics by stirring up "our citizens who have ties of blood" with the peoples of Europe. In spite of Truman's lament, Eisenhower was swept into office on November 4, 1952, with a spectacular plurality of the votes. Virtually all of the one-time isolationist German ethnic vote of the Midwest cascaded into the Eisenhower victory column. Eight years later these same areas held solidly for Republican candidate [Richard] Nixon, though they were highly fragmented by the [Barry] Goldwater debacle in 1964. Seemingly, then, the Republican National Committee's Ethnic Origins Division had done for Eisenhower in 1952 what a less conscious, but similar plan, had done for Truman in 1948.

Successful as the Eisenhower strategy proved to be, it should not be concluded that the German vote alone elected Eisenhower. In fact, it may have been one of the least significant German bloc votes because of Eisenhower's liabilities—the defeat of Germany and the prisoner issue—among German-Americans. Whatever its significance, the German vote has been catered to less and less since 1952. This is phenomenal because as late as the 1950 census, the Germans of foreign birth, or of German-born and mixed parentage living in the United States, still represented the largest foreign white stock in the nation. In 1950 they amounted to 14 percent of the total U. S. population. The only similarly large bloc of foreign stock was the Italians with 13.5 percent. The Polish were a distant third with but 8.3 percent. When looking at the foreign-born only, the Germans in 1950 totaled 984,000, a figure which is second only to the Italians who numbered 1,427,000. Also in 1950 there were 5,000,000 persons in the United States whose mother tongue was German, well over a million more than the Italian speakers, the other large non-English-speaking group in America at that time. Whatever the explanation, the German element grew ever more invisible during the 1950s.

The German-American Community Declines

Several journalists have tried to assess what happened to the German-American community during those years. One, Berlin-born Gerard H. Wilk, an emigré New Yorker since 1946, recorded the words of a German immigrant worker whom he interviewed in New York in 1954: "Those *Vereinsmeier* [club enthusiasts], they keep wishing for a Germany that doesn't exist any more. I can't understand all that gush of theirs. Forever singing about the Rhine, the Main, the Neckar—they live in a vacuum, Herr Wilk; it's neither fish nor fowl, as the saying goes, it's neither Germany nor America. . . . My sons are married, my grandchildren don't know a word of German except for the Christmas songs. I'm satisfied, no regrets."

In Wilk's view, the four or five hundred German clubs in the metropolitan New York area were recruiting their members among the sons and daughters of post–World War I German immigrants. The emphasis was on entertainment, but each organization had its *Herr Präsident* who took his duties seriously and easily developed a consensus in his constituency if he stuck to the standard, well-known festivals and celebrations. Wilk theorized that in one respect, a separatist German-American culture had developed in the United States when the Germans were threatened by [anti-immigrant] Nativism during the 1850s. A century before his time, Wilk contended, the Germans had cut themselves off, founded their own societies, churches, schools, and newspapers and built a wall around their brand of American individualism which slowed their assimilation. Dying a peaceful death after the turn of the century, the feelings of being under siege were rekindled during World War I, but assimilation was hastened, Wilk believed, by Hitler and his propaganda. The Germans in America in the 1950s, according to Wilk wanted no part of politics—any politics, German or American.

Although this explanation may be incomplete, the fact remains that the German vote largely disappeared during the 1950s. There are no longer any German political candidates, no German component in the ethnic structure of any American city's political machine, and seemingly there was no German-American backlash to the desegregation movement during the 1960s. When [social scientists] Nathan Glazer, Andrew Greeley, Michael Novak and others write about American ethnics, they rarely include references to the German element. Today there is only the Anglo-Teutonic white stock, which makes up a segment of America's silent majority. Undoubtedly the German-American voter could be aroused again with a volatile issue, but none is apparent on the horizon.

Due, perhaps, to the economic miracle in [preunification] West Germany, the political restructuring, and the high degree of military and economic cooperation between the United States and Germany, the peoples of both nations feel particularly at ease in communication together. Exchange students in high schools and colleges, marriage partners, and German professionals on temporary assignments in the

United States are welcomed in even the smallest, most conservative American community. German-born scientists hold top positions in the American space program and in government and industry. Perhaps it is significant that the German element did not take particular pride in seeing the Nixon White House and the original Nixon Cabinet packed with men whose names were German—Kleindienst, Haldeman, Ehrlichman, Ziegler, and others—nor were they disillusioned in the slightest when some of these men were convicted for their Watergate crimes. For that matter, while Americans generally laud German-born Secretary of State Henry Kissinger, one seldom hears German-Americans express ethnic pride or a sense of cultural identity with him. In Kissinger's native Germany, however, nearly every citizen hastens to remind one that Kissinger is German-born. . . .

German-Americans Today

Today there is a plethora of German-American organizations, but few of them have broad influence. The Steuben Society, successor of the German-American Alliance, is largely confined to the eastern United States. Only the *Deutsch-Amerikanischer National-Kongress*, known by its abbreviation DANK, has seminational status. Founded in 1958, the congress held its first assembly and was chartered by Illinois in 1959. DANK's goals are unification of German-Americans, friendship between the United States and Germany, preservation of the German language and customs, and the distribution of accurate information to counter-balance false information about the Germans. Its greatest strength is in the Chicago area, but it has affiliates in Wisconsin, Indiana, Ohio, Iowa, Michigan, Minnesota, New Jersey, Arkansas, Pennsylvania, and Washington, D.C. Youth activities, a monthly called *Der Deutsch-Amerikaner*, and travel opportunities round out the program of DANK.

Many cities in the United States continue their German

singing clubs, variously named *Männerchöre* and *Damen-chöre*, but the German mutual aid and gymnastic societies have dwindled to a handful. German-language newspapers, too, have declined. The 140-year-old *New Yorker Staats-Zeitung und Herold* (which publishes regional papers in German) continues its proud tradition, and there are others: The *Amerika Herold* and regional papers published by the Tribune Company of Omaha, the *Chicago Abendpost*, the New York *Aufbau*, the Cincinnati *Kurier*, the Buffalo *Volksfreund*, the *Detroiter Abendpost*, the St. Louis *Deutsche Wochenschrift*, the Milwaukee *Herold* (printed by the Tribune in Omaha), the Cleveland *Wächter und Anzeiger*, the *California Staats-Zeitung* of Los Angeles, the *Plattdütsche Post* of Staten Island, and the New Jersey *Freie Zeitung*. The German, Austrian, and Hungarian societies of Chicago publish the weekly fifteen-page *Eintracht* for the German-language clubs in that city—an indication of the lively German-American community in Chicago.

To the question "What about the German-Americans today?" we might refer to the anecdote of a European who journeyed to the New World in the eighteenth century. Asked what kind of people the Americans were, the traveler replied, "There are no foreigners. Everybody is an American." His answer was both a definition and a prophecy. And yet, curiosity is awakening in younger Americans of German descent.

Perhaps the crux of the revived interest was expressed by a fourth-generation German-American pastor who told me, "We are a strange and rootless bunch. Whatever we are, whether it is Germans trying to be Americans or Americans trying to be Germans, we are all searching for identity." A descendant of Forty-eighters [refugees from the 1848 German Revolution], the man gives Sunday sermons in German—although he has never visited Germany. But he knows history and explains that German-Americans are worse off than other hyphenates in America because their ethnic roots are so fragmented.

The German immigrant until 1870 had no nation, only many German states. Austria-Hungary was a hybrid of many peoples. Those from Luxembourg, Switzerland, Poland, Czechoslovakia, and Russia might be German-speaking, if not German by nationality, and they identified with the German element in the United States. But, according to the youthful pastor, the Germans suffer from one additional identity-shattering bit of history: of all the immigrant groups in the United States, the Germans alone were splintered along religious lines. They were Protestant or Catholic. But Protestant meant Lutheran or Reformed—plus the many sects. Add to the complexity the indigenous regionalism that afflicts Germans everywhere (Prussian vs. Rhinelander, Hamburger vs. Bavarian) and the puzzle becomes insoluble.

German historians in the 1930s expressed sarcasm when they referred to the United States as that "grave of *Deutschtum.*" Implied in the phrase was the truism that German nationalism in the United States is dead and buried. Nationalism has been welcomed in our time as a bulwark against the loss of identity. [Former French president] Charles De Gaulle turned his perception of this fact into political advantage. But not even the wildest dreamer would think of wooing the Germans in America the way De Gaulle courted the French-speaking people of Quebec. The German-Americans who still pursue the German culture in America remind the observer of a great Gatsby.[1] They are marvelous courtly lovers who seek the affection of their lady *Deutschtum* with a passion that is old, less than ardent, and quite out of date. And besides, the ladylove has already passed away.

---

1. the title character from F. Scott Fitzgerald's *The Great Gatsby*, who pines for an old lover

CHAPTER 4

Notable German Americans

COMING TO AMERICA

Levi Strauss, Entrepreneur

Harold Evans, with Gail Buckland and David Lefer

Levi Strauss brought his entrepreneurial spirit with him when he arrived in New York from Bremen, Germany, in 1847. In this selection Harold Evans describes how Strauss traveled west, following his sister and her family to San Francisco in 1853. His plan was to set up a trading business, but he quickly saw a need among the hard-working gold miners for sturdy pants that would withstand the wear and tear they were subjected to in the goldfields. Strauss capitalized on this need. Using fellow immigrant Jacob Davis's invention—the rivet system that strengthened the pants' pockets—Strauss introduced the first blue jeans to America. They immediately became a staple of the workingman's wardrobe. Strauss's invention is still wildly popular today, and his Levi's brand continues to flourish. Evans, a celebrated historian and journalist, is the author of *The American Century* and *They Made America*. This selection is taken from the latter. Buckland is a professor of the history of photography at the Cooper Union in New York City and is the author of several books on the history of photography. Lefer is an investigative journalist.

Fresh off the boat from Bremen in Germany in 1847, 18-year-old Levi Strauss was soon walking the streets of New York laboring under the 100-pound weight of two packs, one on his chest and one on his back. He carried bolts of cloth, yarns, needles, scissors, buttons, combs, books, shoes, blankets and kettles, and he carried them as far out as Pelham in Westchester County, knocking on doors and hoping to make a sale. He picked up a few words of English as he went along. On the road during the week, he slept in barns and stables and ditches. He was always back in lower Manhattan on Friday for the Jewish Sabbath.

Levi had crossed the Atlantic with his mother and three sisters, packed for a month in the cramped and dank quarters of steerage, the latter part on a diet of dried lentils and salt pork when their supply of kosher food ran out. "Levi" was a changed name. His original name of Loeb was all right in German but awkward in English, and he meant to get on in this new world where Jews were treated like everyone else. He had grown up in a village in the forested countryside of Buttenheim in upper Franconia north of Nuremberg, the son of Hirsch, a peddler, and Hirsch's second wife, Rebeccca Hans. It was a beautiful place, but Jewish families were forbidden to own land, limiting them to a few trades like peddling, and the vague threat of pogroms[1] haunted their every day. On the death of their father in 1845, two of Levi's half brothers, Jonas and Louis, immigrated to America and they were busy street peddlers by the time Levi arrived. Jewish peddlers were known and often welcomed across America in the first part of the 19th century. Many Jewish peddlers did well enough to find more lucrative occupations. Some became doctors or other professionals. A few former peddlers, like Benjamin Altman, Adam Gimbel and Meyer Guggenheim, became tycoons.

Chasing the Gold Rush

After three years on the street, Jonas and Louis in 1848 were able to open a small wholesale business at 203½ Di-

---

1. an organized attack on innocent people

vision Street in an area called Hebrew Market, but Levi
had caught the American bug: He was restless. Everyone
in America, it seemed, was forever on the move. Levi's sister Fanny married another Jewish immigrant peddler,
David Stern, and was off to St. Louis, Missouri. Levi went
to live in Louisville and tried his luck humping his brothers' supplies in the Kentucky hills.

He had not been at it long when the whole country was
convulsed by the California gold rush. In 1849 alone,
80,000 prospectors flooded into the state. Soon afterward,
Fanny and David Stern were drawn to San Francisco, and
Levi decided to join them there in a trading partnership.
Before heading out to San Francisco, he went all the way
back to New York to stock up from his brothers' business.
It is indicative of the adventurous character of the boy
from a Bavarian village, and the questing spirit of the age,
that he should undertake the trip loaded up with everything
he imagined California miners might need. There was no
railway across the country. Some went by land, with all its
dangers of thirst and Indian raids; many went by the malar-
ial Isthmus of Panama; others sailed round Cape Horn. All
these routes took tedious and dangerous months. Levi chose
to put his bundles of blankets and spades and boots on a
sailing ship to Panama in the first week of February and
then on the Pacific Mail Steamer *Isthmus* to San Francisco.
He did not disembark until March 14, 1853, just after his
24th birthday and his grant of American citizenship.

San Francisco was a riotous place, 399 saloons and 28
breweries, and 1,200 known murders that year in a population of 70,000, plus another 2,400 newcomers who van-
ished never to be seen again alive. More than 1,000 ghost
ships lay in the harbor, abandoned by crews bitten by the
gold bug. There were already 117 dry-goods stores in the
gold rich but merchandise poor city, where a blanket worth
$5 in New York could fetch $40. Levi and Stern set up a

"dry goods and clothing" wholesale business at 90 Sacramento Street on the pilings close by the wharf. They had an edge on the competition, with supplies assured from Levi's brothers, who now had a large store at 165 Houston Street in New York, but Levi and Stern also posted a boy with a telescope in the San Francisco hills and, on his alert of approaching ships, they bedded down in their warehouse. At dawn, they would rush to the first ship docking to bid for cargo up for auction. Being first onboard was often the difference between a good and a bad week.

A New Idea

It is not entirely clear how Levi came up with the idea for what became his principal product—too many records were lost in the San Francisco earthquake and fire of 1906—but he could hardly have failed to notice that the miners, lumberjacks, teamsters and ranchers on the streets were raggedly clad in trousers with threadbare seats, holed knees and pockets ripped from jamming in gold nuggets, gloves, tools. Legend has it a miner complained: "Should'a brought pants. Pants don't wear worth a hoot in the diggin's. Can't get a pair strong enough to last." The story goes that Levi then tailored a pair of pants from canvas intended for a Conestoga wagon. It is not likely given that he was a wholesaler supplying retailers, and he would not have had tailors on the premises. Who it was who cut the first hard-wearing denim pants and in what style is unknown to history, but when the pants arrived (the material probably from the New York warehouse), we do know that Levi sold them as "waist high overalls." The miner in the myth is said to have paid in gold dust worth six dollars. Certainly his affection for them became widely known. More men went into stores asking for the same waist-high overalls. His brothers sent Levi blue denim, twill weave durable cotton, which he passed on to outside tailors to cut and sew.

The work pants soon became the center of a flourishing wholesale store, and Levi began his lifelong tradition of philanthropy. The Orphan Asylum society of San Francisco records a donation of five dollars in 1854. When a major banking crisis in 1855 closed businesses, Levi kept in the black by adventuring into the mining camps in the hills above Sacramento. (Leland Stanford, one of four merchant-progenitors of the transcontinental railway, had plied the same routes.) The partners hired traveling salesmen as trade revived and moved into successively larger premises; in 1857 Levi's half-brother, Louis, came out from New York to help. In February 1861 it was recorded that the company sent no less than $59,732.24 worth of gold to New York to pay for supplies. In 1866 Levi spent $25,000 to adorn new headquarters of Levi Strauss and Co. at 14–16 Battery Street with gaslight chandeliers, a cast-iron front and one of the first freight elevators. He dealt in fancier goods now, Irish linen and Belgian lace and Italian shawls along with blankets and women's clothing and the rugged work clothes. The store would no doubt have continued that way, successful but unexceptional, but for a remarkable congruence seized and exploited by Levi.

Strauss Takes a Partner

Another Jewish immigrant, who had come to America some seven years after Levi, changed his name and come west, was struggling to make a living in Reno, Nevada. Jacob Youphes, born in Riga [Latvia] in 1831, was now Jacob Davis. In 16 years of roving North America, he had failed as a tailor, a miner, a brewer and a tobacconist, and was trying his luck again as a tailor. He lived in a shack by the recently finished transcontinental railroad track making a few horse blankets, wagon covers and tents. In December 1870 the wife of a woodcutter asked him to make pants that would not rip. The strongest material Jacob had was ten-ounce duck twill, which he usually used for making tents. When the wife came with three dollars and the woodcutter's measurements, Jacob sat cross-legged on his bench and sewed the heavy, hard-to-cut cloth while she waited. He fussed with the stitches because he knew that many workmen's clothes tore at the pockets. Some rivets lay on the table. He routinely used them to hold horse blankets together. The thought just struck him, he testified later in a patent "to fasten the pockets with those rivets." He hammered them into the corners of the back and front pockets, and later watched the riveted woodcutter trudge into the hills with his ax over his shoulder. "I did not make a big thing of it," he told the court during one of many later patent suits. "I sold those pants and never thought of it for a time."

The next month four men came to Jacob's shack for riveted pants. In February 1871 he sold ten pairs and in March a surveying party bought a dozen. Men who wore them were walking advertisements. After 18 months he had sold 200 pairs in white duck cloth or blue denim. The hand-to-mouth Jacob had been able to buy the initial material only because his supplier was a trusting soul: Levi Strauss. He habitually let hardworking customers run up a line of credit. Jacob recognized the value of his little invention, but it cost money he did not have to apply for a patent; his wife, Annie, told him not to waste any more of their money on such madcap schemes, since he already had two patents and the couple were still poor. So it was that on July 2, 1872, the inventor wrote to Levi with a proposition. His German was still better than his English, and his letter, which he dictated to the town druggist, reflected the inflections of his Eastern European Jewish accent:

> The secret of them Pents is the Rivits that I put in those
> Pockets and I found the demand so large that I cannot
> make them up fast enough. I charge for the Duck $3.00
> and the Blue $2.50 a pear. My nabors are getting yealouse

of these success and unless I secure it by Patent Papers it will soon become a general thing. Everybody will make them up and there will be no money in it.

Therefore Gentlemen, I wish to make you a Proposition that you should take out the Latters Patent in my name as I am the inventor of it, the expense of it will be about $68, all complit and for these $68 I will give you half the right to sell all such clothing Revited according to the Patent, for all the Pacific States and Teroterious, the balince of the United States and half of the Pacific Coast I resarve for myself. The invesment for you is but a trifle compaired with the improvement in all Coarst Clothing. I use it in all Blankit Clothing such as Coats, Vests and Pents, and you will find it a very salable article at a much advents rate. . . .

These looks like a trifle hardley worth speakeing off but nevertheless I knew you can make a very large amount of money on it. If you make pents the way I do you can sell Duck Pents such as the Sample at $30 per doz. And they will readly retail for $3 a pair.

A Patent for Rivets

Pants that could fetch $30 a dozen wholesale were gold dust. Levi's company pants sold for only $10 a dozen. A baser person than Levi Strauss would not have hesitated to steal Jacob's idea—the patent suits are populated by such scoundrels—but Levi accepted Jacob's offer. He paid for a patent application on behalf of Davis and Levi Strauss and Co. for "improvement in fastening seams . . . in order to prevent the seam from starting or giving away from the frequent strain or pressure." The Patent Office rejected the application. It was considered too similar to other patents using rivets to hold together clothing. Rivets had been used on soldiers' boots during the Civil War. Levi paid for ten months of haggling over wording, and three amendments later, Jacob and Levi had their patent—139,121—approved on May 20, 1873.

Jacob, back in Reno, had meanwhile been trying to sell pants on his own, with only a handful of orders. He realized he needed the superior business skills, literacy and capital of Levi; and the two men of roughly the same age—Levi was 44, Jacob 42—got on well. On April 26, 1873, a month before the patent was finally approved, Jacob sold his half share of it to Levi Strauss and Company, closed his railroad-side shop and moved with Annie and their six children to a good house in a fashionable district of San Francisco to begin a new salaried life as the head tailor and foreman of production. A devastating depression started in 1873, but the first blue jeans started running wild after the first sale in June. By the end of the year, the company had earned $43,510. No fewer than 20,000 men were out on the streets and in the hills sporting their Levi Strauss pants with a distinctive orange seam thread that Jacob had introduced to match the color of the rivets. Davis was running himself ragged, supervising the cutting of the blue denim and its delivery to individual seamstresses, so Levi decided demand was not best met by dispersed workers. Risking a fair amount of capital, he set up a factory in Fremont Street with 60 seamstresses on the spot, each one sewing a complete pair of pants from 15 pieces of cloth. The best could make five pairs a day, earning $3, the same level of earnings as a bricklayer or mechanic. It represented an increase in productivity, though not as much as would have been achieved by the American system, popular in the East, of dividing the work process into very small, specialized tasks. Levi could have cut his costs by employing cheaper Chinese labor (as Charles Crocker had done building the Central Pacific). Whether Levi shared the general xenophobia or just thought it good business is unclear, but he made a point of advertising his discrimination: "Our riveted goods . . . are made up in our Factory, under our direct supervision, and by WHITE LA-

BOR only." Levi's campaign lasted until the 20th century. (He did employ one Chinese man, to perform the exacting job of cutting denim and duck canvas with a long knife. It took strength to cut through the layers of cloth and endurance to do nothing but that all day. Every white worker hired for the job had quit.) . . .

Sales Keep Climbing

By 1876 sales had climbed to $200,000 a year. Sales representatives traveled to Mexico, Hawaii, Tahiti and New Zealand. By 1880 the company had 250 workers and sales of $2.4 million. A decade later, the total was 450 workers, with an additional 85 employees in the offices. The pants had become *the* western dress code. Levi relished the way his clothing served the needs of the workingman. He emphasized it in his advertising: "These goods are especially adapted for the use of FARMERS, MECHANICS, MINERS and WORKING MEN in general." He had a guarantee sewn on to the back of the pants promising "a new pair FREE" if the current pair ripped. The picture of two horses trying to pull apart a pair of pants became a trademark. Infringers of the original patent were thwarted in successful court actions. The Levi's (as they became known early in the 20th century) were valued for their strength, but they were also on the way to becoming a symbol of democratic equality.

Levi was a millionaire several times over by then, but he had no time for mere accumulation. In his only known interview, in 1895, at the age of 66, he told the *San Francisco Bulletin*: "My happiness lies in my routine work. . . . I do not think large fortunes cause happiness to their owners, for immediately those who possess them become slaves to their wealth. They must devote their lives to caring for their possessions. I don't think money brings friends to its owner. In fact, often the result is quite contrary."

Louis Strauss died in San Francisco in 1881 and Jonas

in New York in 1886. In that year, only 12 years after David Stern's death, Levi stepped back from his day-to-day role, handing the burden to Fanny's four sons, Jacob, Sigmund, Louis, and Abraham. He and his nephews officially incorporated the company in 1890, the year that the lot number "501R" was first used to designate the denim waist overalls—and the year the patent ran out, freeing others to imitate the design. Levi remained active in philanthropy as a trustee of the Pacific Hebrew Orphan Asylum and Home and the Eureka Benevolent Society. He established 28 perpetual scholarships to the University of California, four from each congressional district in the state. On his death at the age of 73 in 1901, he left much to Hebrew and Roman Catholic orphanages and the Emanu-El Sisterhood, but most of his $6 million went to his four nephews, as Fanny had hoped. The Stern brothers ran the business for years after their uncle's death, and then it passed to Sigmund Stern's son-in-law, Walter Haas, and his family. Robert Haas and his uncle Peter, leaders of the firm in 2003, are the fifth generation of Levi Strauss's extended family to own and run the company.

A Legacy Endures

Levi achieved immortality with his jeans—though jeans is a word he never used. It was not until the 1960s, 60 years after his death, that the company came to use the term. They were still essentially western wear, with only 10 percent of sales in the East until the 1950s. But as a universal popular culture emanated from Hollywood, something happened to transform Levi's from clothing into a ubiquitous cultural statement all around the world, one of independence, rebellion, equality, freedom. It began in the '30s, when the West truly captured America's and the world's imagination through the movies. Levi's came to be associated less with rough labor and more with the romance of the free-roaming cowboy. Each generation since, from World War II to the rebellious '60s, and the leisure era, has vested Levi's with mythic qualities. *Life* magazine noted the effect in 1974, when U.S. production of 450 million yards of denim a year could not keep up with demand: "The jeans that once encased the scrawny rumps of cowboys and gold miners of the American West have become the standard garb of the world's youth. They're the favorite off-duty clothes of fashion models from L.A. to St. Tropez. By buying up bales of fashionably tattered used ones, Britain and the Continent have made millionaire exporters of U.S. ragmen."

Seventy-five million pairs of genuine Levi's were sold that year; they were copied more than any other piece of clothing. How curious that a long-dead poor immigrant should be hailed as a world leader of fashion. It is a commentary on the social attitudes of the time that in England the men whose names came to be commemorated in clothing were aristocrats—Cardigan, Wellington and Raglan—but in America it was a street peddler of workaday clothes.

Albert Einstein, Physicist

Abraham Pais

Albert Einstein is best known for his theory of relativity. But he made many other contributions to the world of physics, including a proposal outlining the existence of light quanta and the photo-electric effect, for which he received the Nobel Prize in 1922. In this selection fellow physicist Abraham Pais describes Einstein's early days, his academic and professional careers, and his immigration to the United States when the Nazis came to power in 1933. Pais, who died in 2000, was a renowned theoretical physicist and scientific historian. He also authored a full-length biography of Einstein, *Subtle Is the Lord: The Science and Life of Albert Einstein*. This selection was excerpted from his book *The Genius of Science: A Portrait Gallery*.

Albert Einstein, this century's [the 1900s] most renowned scientist, was born in Ulm, in the kingdom of Württemberg, now part of Germany, the son of Hermann Einstein, a small businessman, never very successful, and Pauline née Koch. In 1881 Maria, his only sibling, was born. In 1880 the family moved to Munich, where Einstein attended public school and high school, always doing well. (The story that he was a poor pupil is a myth, probably caused by his dislike of formal education.) In those years he also received violin lessons privately and, in order to comply with legal requirements, instruction in the elements of Judaism. As a result of this inculcation, Einstein went through an intense religious phase at age about eleven, following religious precepts in detail and (he later told a friend) composing songs in honor of God. A year later, this phase ended abruptly and forever as a result of his exposure to popular books on science, to 'the holy geometry book' (as he called it) on Euclidean geometry, to the writings of [philosopher Immanuel] Kant, and more.

An Unorthodox Higher Education

In 1895 Einstein took the entrance examination at the Federal Institute of Technology (ETH) in Zurich but failed because of poor grades in literary and political history. In 1896, after a year of study at a high school in Aarau (Switzerland), he did gain admission, however. In that year he gave up his German citizenship and became stateless, in 1901, Swiss.

During his next four years as an ETH student, Einstein did not excel in regular course attendance, relying far more on self-study. In 1900 he passed his final examinations with good grades, which qualified him as a high school teacher in mathematics and physics. For the next two years he had to be satisfied with temporary teaching positions until, in June 1902, he was appointed technical expert third class at the Patent Office in Berne.

In January 1903 Einstein married Mileva Maric, of Greek-Catholic Serbian descent, a fellow student at the ETH. In 1902 the couple had a daughter out of wedlock, Lieserl, whose fate remains unknown, and after marriage two sons, Hans Albert, who became a distinguished professor of hydraulic engineering in Berkeley, California, and Eduard, a gifted child, who became a student of medicine in Zurich, but then turned severely schizophrenic and died in a psychiatric hospital.

In 1914 the Einsteins separated, in 1919 they divorced.

Thereafter Einstein remarried with his cousin Elsa Einstein, who brought him two stepdaughters. He had several extramarital affairs during this second marriage.

Emerging Genius

None of Einstein's first four papers, published between 1901 and 1904, fore-shadowed his explosive creativity of 1905, his *annus mirabilis* [miraculous year], in which he produced: in March, his proposal of the existence of light quanta and the photo-electric effect, work for which in 1922 he received the Nobel Prize; in April, a paper on the determination of molecular dimensions which earned him his PhD in Zurich; in May, his theory of special relativity; in September, a sequel to the preceding paper containing the relation $E = mc^2$. Any one of these papers would have made him greatly renowned; their totality made him immortal.

Only after all these publications did Einstein's academic career begin: privat-dozent [post-doctoral teacher] in Berne, 1908; associate professor, University of Zurich, 1909, the year of his first honorary degree (Geneva); full professor at the Karl Ferdinand University, Prague, 1911; professor at the ETH, 1912; professor and member of the Prussian Academy of Sciences, Berlin, 1914–32, where he arrived four months before the outbreak of the First World War.

In 1915 Einstein cosigned his first political document, a 'Manifesto to Europeans,' in which all those who cherish European culture were urged to join in a League of Europeans (never realized). Far more important, in that year Einstein completed his masterpiece, perhaps the most profound contribution to physics of the twentieth century: his general relativity theory, on which he had been brooding for the previous eight years. In the special theory all laws of physics have the same form for any two observers moving relatively to each other in a straight line and with constant, time-independent, velocity. In the general theory the same is true for *all* kinds of relative motion. This demands a revision of Newton's thory of gravitation. Space is curved, Einstein now asserted, the amount of curvature depending on how dense matter is at that place—matter determines by its gravitational action 'what shape space is in.'

The superiority of Einstein's over Newton's theory became manifest in 1915, when Einstein could for the first time explain an anomaly in the motion of the planet Mercury (advance of the perihelion), known observationally since 1859. He also predicted that light grazing the sun bends by a factor two larger than predicted by Newton's theory.

Achieving Mythical Status

In 1916 Einstein completed his most widely known book *On the Special and the General Theory of Relativity, Popularly Explained*, wrote the first paper on gravitational waves and became president of the *Deutsche Physikalische Gesellschaft* [German Physicist Society]. In 1917 he became ill, suffering successively from a liver ailment, a stomach ulcer, jaundice, and general weakness, but nevertheless managed to complete his first paper on relativistic cosmology. He did not fully recover until 1920.

In November 1919 Einstein became the mythical figure he is to this day. In May of that year two solar eclipse expeditions had (in the words of the astronomer [Arthur] Eddington) 'confirmed Einstein's weird theory of non-Euclidean space.' On November 6, the President of the Royal Society declared in London that this was 'the most remarkable scientific event since the discovery [in 1846] of the predicted existence of the planet Neptune.'

The next day *The Times* in London carried an article headlined 'Revolution in Science/New theory of the Universe/Newtonian ideas overthrown.' Einstein had triumphed over Newton (who of course is and remains a stellar figure in science). The drama of that moment was enhanced by the contrast with the recently concluded World War, which had caused millions to die, empires to fall, the future to be uncertain. At that time Einstein emerges, bringing new law and order. From that time on the world press made him into an icon, . . . the divine man, of the twentieth century.

A Change of Focus

At about that time one begins to perceive changes in the activities of Einstein, now in mid-life. He began writing non-scientific articles. In 1920 he was exposed to anti-semitic demonstrations during a lecture he gave in Berlin. At the same time, Jews fleeing from the East came literally knocking at his door for help. All that awakened in Einstein a deepened awareness of the Jewish predicament, and caused him to speak up and write in favor of Jewish self-expression by means of settling in Palestine, creating there a peaceful center where Jews could live in dignity and without persecution. Thus, he became an advocate of what one may call moral Zionism, though he never was a member of any Zionist organization.

The 1920s was also the period of Einstein's most extensive travels. In 1921 he paid his first visit to the United States for the purpose of raising funds for the planned Hebrew University, being honored on the way, including being received by President [Warren G.] Harding. In 1922 his visit to Paris contributed to the normalization of Franco-German relations. Also in that year he accepted membership in the League of Nations' Committee on Intellectual Cooperation. In June, Walter Rathenau, Foreign Minister of Germany, a Jew and an acquaintance of Einstein, was assassinated. After being warned that he, too, might be in danger, Einstein left with his wife for a five months' trip abroad. After short visits to Colombo, Singapore, Hong Kong, and Shanghai, they arrived in Japan for a five-week stay. The press reported that, at a reception, the center of attention was not the Empress, everything turned on Einstein.

On the way back they visited Palestine. In introducing Einstein at a lecture, the president of the Zionist Executive said: 'Mount the platform which has been awaiting you for two thousand years.' Thereafter Einstein spent three weeks in Spain. In 1925 he journeyed to South America, lecturing in Buenos Aires, Montevideo, and Rio de Janeiro. Apart from three later trips to the United States, this was the last major voyage in Einstein's life.

More Contributions to Physics

All these multifarious activities took a lot of Einstein's energies but did not keep him from his physics research. In 1922 he published his first paper on unified field theory, an attempt at incorporating not only gravitation but also electromagnetism into a new world geometry, a subject that was his main concern until the end of his life. He tried many approaches; none of them have worked out. In 1924 he published three papers on quantum statistical mechanics which include his discovery of so-called Bose-Einstein condensation. This was his last contribution to physics which may be called seminal. He did continue to publish all through his later years, however.

In 1925 quantum mechanics arrived, a new theory with which Einstein never found peace. His celebrated dialogue with [Niels] Bohr on this topic started at the 1927 Solvay conference. They were to argue almost until Einstein's death without ever coming to an agreement.

In 1928 Einstein suffered a temporary physical collapse due to an enlargement of the heart. He had to stay in bed for four months and keep to a salt-free diet. He fully recuperated but stayed weak for a year. 1929 witnessed his first visit with the Belgian royal family, leading to a life-long correspondence with Queen Elizabeth.

Settling in the United States

Einstein had been a pacifist since his young years but in the 1920s his position became more radical in this respect. For example, in 1925 he, [Mohandas K.] Gandhi, and others signed a manifesto against obligatory military service, in 1930 another supporting world government. In that year and again in 1931 he visited the United States. In 1932 he accepted appointment as professor at the Institute for Advanced Study in Princeton, originally intending to divide his time between Princeton and Berlin. When, however, he and his wife left Germany on December 10 of that year, they would never set foot in Germany again—in January 1933 the Nazis came to power. Though remaining pacifist at heart, Einstein was deeply convinced that they could only be defeated by the force of arms.

Because of the new political situation, Einstein changed his plans, arriving on October 17, 1933, in the US to settle permanently in Princeton, whereafter he left that country only once, in 1935, to travel to Bermuda in order to make from there application for permanent residency. In 1940 he became a US citizen.

Einstein also remained a prominent figure in his new country. In 1934 he and his wife were invited by the Roosevelts and spent a night at the White House. He remained scientifically active, wrote in fact some good papers, but nothing as memorable as in his European days.

In 1939 Einstein wrote to [Franklin Delano] Roosevelt to draw his attention to possible military uses of atomic energy. His influence on these later developments was marginal, however. In 1943 he became consultant to the US Navy Bureau of Ordnance but was never involved in atomic bomb work. In 1944 a copy of his 1905 paper on relativity,

handwritten by him for this purpose, was auctioned for six
million dollars as a contribution to the war effort. (It is now
in the Library of Congress.) After the war he continued to
speak out on political issues, such as his open letter to the
United Nations urging the formation of a world government, and his frequent condemnations in the press of [Sen.
Joseph] McCarthy's [anti-Communist] activities. After the
death of Chaim Weizmann, first president of Israel, Einstein was invited, but declined, to be his successor.

In 1948 Einstein was found to have a large intact
aneurysm of the abdominal aorta. In 1950 he wrote his testament, willing his papers and manuscripts to the Hebrew
University (where they are now). On April 11, 1955, Einstein wrote his last letter (to [philosopher] Bertrand Russell), in which he agreed to sign a manifesto urging all nations to renounce nuclear weapons. On April 13 Einstein
wrote a draft (incomplete) for a radio address which ends:
'Political passions, aroused everywhere, demand their victims.' On the afternoon of that day his aneurysm rup-
tured. On the 15th he entered Princeton Hospital, where
he died on April 18 at 1:15 A.M. His body was cremated
that same day. The ashes were scattered at an undisclosed
place. The following November his first great-grandson
was born.

Dr. Seuss, Children's Author

Ruth K. MacDonald

Theodor Geisel, better known as Dr. Seuss, has captivated several generations of school-age children with his whimsical books and characters. In this selection, written three years before Dr. Seuss' death in 1991, Ruth K. MacDonald discusses the early influences on his writing, including his feelings of shame at his German heritage during World War I. The author tracks Dr. Seuss through his formative years and reveals the inspiration for his many children's books. MacDonald taught English at New Mexico State University. She is also the author of *Literature for Children in England and America, 1646–1774* and *Dr. Seuss*, the source of this selection.

Dr. Seuss was born Theodor Seuss Geisel, the only child of Theodor Robert and Henrietta Seuss Geisel. Born on 2 March 1904 in Springfield, Massachusetts, the boy was later educated in the Springfield public school system. Though details of his early life are sketchy, two stand out. He reports remembering reading and drawing constantly, beginning his reading career with [Charles] Dickens and [Robert Louis] Stevenson. The impulse to doodle appeared as early as the impulse to read, though he never had any art training. The extent of his formal art education was a single drawing lesson in high school, which did not encourage his

Ruth K. MacDonald, ed., "From Doodles to Doctorates: The Care and Feeding of a Picture-Book Author," *Dr. Seuss*. Boston: Twayne's United States Authors Series, 1988. Copyright © 1988 by G.K. Hall & Co. All rights reserved. Reproduced by permission of The Gale Group.

own style or method of composition. He walked out of the class and never returned. The other detail worth noting is his feeling of shame at his German heritage during World War I. Nicknamed the Kaiser, and sometimes called the Drunken Kaiser, since the senior Geisel was part owner and eventual president of a brewery, Kuhlmbach and Geisel, the boy was occasionally pelted by rocks as he made his way to and from school. From this feeling of social ostracism may derive that need for privacy and avoidance of crowds that now typifies his life [in 1988].

His Father Was an Enduring Influence

The one clear influence on his early life was his father; the dedication of two of his most successful books indicates the lasting impression that his father had on him. The dedication of *If I Ran the Circus* reads, "Big Ted . . . the Finest Man I'll ever know"; *McElligot's Pool* is also dedicated to his father. Theodor Robert Geisel worked in his brewery for many years, until he finally became its president, ironically on the same day that Prohibition was declared. Undaunted, he took on the job of superintendent of parks for Springfield, a job that included supervising the local zoo. Much has been made of this possible influence on the future Dr. Seuss, but it is important to note that his father did not become connected with the zoo until Seuss was well into his teens. The many reported visits to the zoo of the young boy are erroneous, and the influence is quite tangential. But Seuss did take one lesson from his father's disappointment as a brewmaster—that perseverance in finding another occupation, and doing it well, is the best way to conduct a life.

In his longtime home on Soledad Hill in La Jolla, California, Dr. Seuss has displayed two mementos from his father. The first is a gift from his father, a plaster casting of a huge dinosaur track found in Springfield. From this huge reminder of an extinct species the son interprets that "he was trying to tell me, in joke form, a species can disappear but still leave a track in the sand," a sign to the son not only to make something of his life but also to leave something important behind after his death. The second memento is a paper target from a rifle-shooting contest, marked by five bull's-eyes. This is the target that his father shot at to win a world championship in target shooting. Though Dr. Seuss admits that target shooting has no appeal for him, he does emulate his father's perseverance and his quest for perfection. Seuss admits he has never achieved the latter virtue, though his father's example keeps him trying. This restless striving for perfection has led to a life of disciplined writing and drawing, even at a point in life where other successful writers might have slowed down. But Dr. Seuss works an eight-hour day every day, and finds himself ill at ease when he has nothing to do during vacations.

Though Henrietta Geisel's influence is less direct, it is her maiden name her son borrowed as his pseudonym. Although it is pronounced *Soyce* in German, most English speakers pronounce it as it looks, approximating the pronunciation of *Zeus*, the Olympian suggestiveness perhaps influencing the son's choice of names. Seuss began using the pseudonym during his editorship of the Dartmouth College humor magazine. One source claims that the pseudonym became useful when the young collegian was found with a bottle of gin in his dormitory room and was ordered to relinquish the editorship. The pseudonym simply covered up his continued participation in the magazine's publication. But the author himself claims that he used the name for his humorous essays and drawings, saving the name Geisel for the more serious novels he had planned for himself, but which have never materialized beyond an unpublished manuscript of a virtually undecipherable, stream-of-consciousness novel written in his mid-twenties.

Not a Dedicated Student

After high school, Geisel went to Dartmouth, graduating in 1925. His editorship of and contributions to the college humor magazine, *Jack O'Lantern*, occupied much of his time, since he contributed both cartoons and humorous essays. In later life he has credited his Latin studies in high school and college as influential on his writing, since *Latin* teaches the derivation of words and, he claims, a respect and love for language. "It allows you to adore words—take them apart and find out where they come from." This analysis of words is characteristic of the author's writing, not only in the extreme consistency with which he uses language in children's books—if something falls down, it must have come from someplace up—but also in his made-up words, which sound like real words because they have linguistic markers, as genuine nouns, verbs, and adjectives do.

He was not an honor student, though he made respectable grades, respectable enough to allow him to apply for a fellowship to Oxford. He told his father of his application for the fellowship, which the father duly reported to the local newspaper as having been awarded to Seuss already. When the son failed to win the fellowship, his father felt forced to send him to Oxford anyway, in order to save face. Geisel went to Oxford in the fall of 1925, with the avowed purpose of earning a doctorate in literature and becoming a college professor. His notebooks from the lectures he attended at the time reveal his intentions, for they are filled with doodles rather than notes, suggesting his increasing frustration with his studies: "The astonishing irrelevance of graduate work in English, the committing to memory, for instance of all the vowel changes in Old English . . . had daunted but not defeated me." At the end of a year's study, he conferred with his academic advisor, Emile Legouis, a respected scholar of Jonathan Swift's work. Legouis suggested that Geisel might research Swift's literary output between ages sixteen and seventeen, to see if he actually wrote anything then. If Geisel discovered something, he could write his dissertation on it, earn his doctorate, and ensure his reputation as a literary scholar; if he found nothing, no dissertation, no doctorate, no reputation.

Faced with possible failure after what would be much effort, and disinclined to pursue his studies anyway, Geisel abandoned his studies and went on a tour of Europe. Though clearly no longer an academician, the influence of these Studies in English literature is still clear in Dr. Seuss's work, especially in the early literary fairy tales *The Five Hundred Hats of Bartholomew Cubbins, The Seven Lady Godivas, The King's Stilts,* and *Bartholomew and the Oobleck,* which all show his familiarity with the English folk tale. And though memorizing the vowel changes in Old English may have been tedious, his obvious ability to manipulate the English language has made the author famous and has proved one of Dr. Seuss's greatest assets.

The one piece of evidence about Geisel's mother from the biographies is her response to his status as an Oxford dropout: she "said she was so happy that I would never be a stuffed shirt," an unlikely situation, given the son's satiric and irreverent attitude toward almost everything, revealed in his doodles and essays.

Marriage and Career

The other great influence on his life at the time was his future wife, Helen Palmer, a fellow student at Oxford, who urged him to follow his natural inclinations away from academia. Geisel spent the next year roaming around Europe, studying at the Sorbonne and attempting to write the Great American Novel—albeit with long passages in Spanish, a language he did not understand, which led to long, unintelligible passages. After the year, Geisel returned to the United States and married Palmer in November 1927.

Throughout his varied career as commercial cartoonist, writer of military films, foreign correspondent, documentary writer, and, finally, children's-book writer, he was encouraged and supported by Palmer, who virtually became his manager, helping him run the Beginner Books division of Random House.

The couple had no children; Dr. Seuss is frequently quoted as saying, "You have 'em, I'll amuse 'em," a flip evasion of questions about his childless state. But he credits his isolation from children of his own for keeping him loyal to his own impulses about what makes a good children's book: "If I had children, I'd have been a failure as an author. I would have sought my children's advice about my manuscripts and they would have told me all sorts of fallacious things. And I would have listened." Like many writers for children, Dr. Seuss claims to write to please himself, a formula that succeeds because of Seuss's recognition of the child in himself.

Geisel and his new wife went to New York after their marriage, where he made a living contributing essays and cartoons to such now extinct weekly and monthly magazines as *PM, Judge Liberty, Vanity Fair,* and the early *Life;* and to such ongoing magazines as *Redbook* and *Saturday Evening Post.* In these contributions, a sample of which has been collected by Richard Marschall in *The Tough Coughs as He Ploughs the Dough,* the reader finds a racy, even lewd, sense of humor, which one does not associate with the Dr. Seuss of children's books. The viewer also notes an assemblage of made-up beasts, many of whom reappear, some with virtually no alteration, in later Seuss menageries. Above all, the reader is aware of a sensibility that listens carefully to language in its daily use, and pays careful attention to people's foibles and unexamined notions, and to political, if now obscure, events, all of which were grist to be milled and mixed up into Seussian machines, animals, and jokes in his later children's books. In his introduction to the collection, Marschall places Seuss in the humor traditions of S.J. Perelman and Rube Goldberg, in that all are contemporaries, intentionally ridiculous in their humor, and self-deprecating. It was at the end of his magazine contributions, in 1937, in Judge, that the "Dr." title was added to Seuss, after having been used with Garibaldi, Theophrastus, and Yogi as pseudonyms for Theodor Geisel. The misappropriation of the degree, Dr. Seuss has quipped, saved his father thousands of dollars.

Geisel continued these contributions through 1937, though in 1928 he became an advertising cartoonist for Standard Oil of New Jersey and originated the promotional campaign for an insecticide called Flit. Standard Oil offered a contract after two cartoons. The most famous is titled "Mediaeval Tenant" and shows a dragon preying on a knight in bed, who quips: "Darn it all, another Dragon. And just after I'd sprayed the whole castle with Flit!" The second Flit cartoon is captioned, "The exterminator-man forgets himself at a flea-circus," and shows the exterminator applying Flit to the circus. After these demonstrations of humor and free advertising, Seuss was hired, for the luxurious salary of $12,000 a year, to continue a series of cartoons featuring Flit as the butt of the joke. The refrain, "Quick, Henry, the Flit!,", became a common household phrase. The contract with Standard Oil forbade a number of other commercial ventures that Seuss might have occupied himself with, having found that his work with Flit required only a few days a week. Seuss's lawyer discovered a loophole: the contract did not forbid writing a children's book for publication.

Children's Books

In 1936, after a particularly rough ocean crossing from France to New York aboard the S.S. *Kungsholm*, Geisel was haunted by the ship's engines and their anapestic rhythm. Instead of trying to forget the noise, he found himself composing a story in verse that would fill out the line, "And to think that I saw it on Mulberry Street." The boy Marco's tall tale evolved into a story with illustrations, which was subsequently turned down by twenty-seven publishers, since no one was willing to experiment with a book without precedent in the children's book market at the time. An old college friend who had just been appointed children's editor at Vanguard met Geisel on the street in New York and asked him what he had been doing; a glance at the manuscript resulted in a visit to Vanguard's offices and a signed contract for the book within an hour. . . .

By 1954, when John Hersey's article on the failures of reading instruction in American schools called upon Dr. Seuss to try his hand at a replacement for the basal reader, Geisel was ready to take on the job. In *On Beyond Zebra!*, published in 1955, he ridicules the limitations imposed by traditional school learning, priming the pump for his most famous book, *The Cat in the Hat*, published in 1957, where Dr. Seuss jubilantly breaks the barriers of the basal reader's simplistic language and pedestrian artwork.

It took Geisel over a year to write the book, though he originally thought it might take just a few weeks, given what he remembered about rapidly turning out film scripts during the war. But finding a story and then telling it, using the vocabulary list for beginner books supplied by Houghton Mifflin, proved more difficult than he thought. The book was finally published simultaneously as a textbook by Houghton Mifflin and as a trade book by Random House.

It was a huge success, not only because of its strong story and characterization, but also because it could be published cheaply while still maintaining the quality of the artwork. An improvement in the technique of offset lithography permitted mass merchandising of the book. Without this success, Dr. Seuss would have remained a minor light in the history of children's books. The success prompted Bennett Cerf, then editor at Random House, to claim that Dr. Seuss was the only real genius published on his list, though at the time that list included John O'Hara and William Faulkner.

The Cat in the Hat led to the establishment of the Beginner Books division of Random House, of which Geisel has been president since its inception. Geisel, with much help from his wife, helped to develop the list of picture books suitable for beginning readers. . . .

Awards and Achievements

Though the Beginner Books might not all have been of the quality of Dr. Seuss's other books, they made the public increasingly aware of the author's achievements as a writer. Dartmouth's granting of an honorary doctor of humane letters degree in 1956 made an "honest man" out of the author, who had earlier simply appropriated the title. This was the first in a long line of degrees honoring a lifetime of contribution to children's literature. Honorary doctorates followed from American International College in Springfield, Massachusetts, in 1968; Lake Forest College, Illinois, in 1977; Whittier College, California, in 1980; J. F. Kennedy University, Orinda, California, in 1983; Princeton University, in 1985; and the University of Hartford, Connecticut, in 1986. Seuss also received the Roger Revelle Award, equivalent to an honorary doctorate, from the University of California, San Diego, in 1978. The degrees from Whittier and Kennedy were doctor of literature degrees, indicating a particular appreciation for Dr. Seuss's accomplishments in verse; the degree from Princeton, a doctor of fine arts, honors his illustration with the distinction of a degree.

Other honors followed, including Dr. Seuss Day, proclaimed by the governors of Alabama, Arkansas, California, Delaware, Georgia, Kansas, Minnesota, and Utah, to celebrate his seventy-seventh birthday on 2 March 1981. The Laura Ingalls Wilder Award from the Association for Library Service to Children of the American Library Association honored Dr. Seuss in 1980 for "lasting and substantial contribution to children's literature," perhaps in lieu of all the Newbery awards he did not receive from this same organization. The Regina Medal from the Catholic Library Association in 1982 honors his books for the simple criterion of "excellence." Also in this year followed a Special Award for Distinguished Service to Children from the National Association of Elementary School Principals. Along the way to collecting all these awards Dr. Seuss also received the first Outstanding California Author Award from the California Association of Teachers of English in 1976, a Peabody Award for his television specials "How the Grinch Stole Christmas" and "Horton Hears a Who" in 1971, Emmy Awards in 1977 for "Halloween is Grinch Night" and 1982 for "The Grinch Grinches the Cat in the Hat," and finally, a Pulitzer Prize in 1984 "for his contribution over nearly half a century to the education and enjoyment of America's children and their parents." The attention these awards brought to the normally reclusive author has made him uncomfortable, though not so much so that he was scared away from a birthday celebration in 1986 in New York to celebrate the release of his adult book *You're Only Old Once! A Book for Obsolete Children.*

Not all the attention has been positive. With the publication of *The Butter Battle Book* in 1984, which took on the issue of imminent nuclear disaster, critics charged Dr. Seuss with a number of heinous crimes against childhood: oversimplifying the issue; frightening children; introducing them to subject matter they did not need to know about until they were older; vilifying the effectiveness of nuclear deterrence; and frustrating children with the open, unresolved ending. In spite of the response of the critics, the book made the juvenile best-seller list in the *New York Times* and praise from many groups, especially nuclear disarmament activists.

The death of Helen Palmer Geisel in 1967, Geisel's re-marriage to Audrey Stone Diamond in 1968, advancing age, and his sometimes precarious health—a heart attack, cancer surgery, and cataract surgery—have at times slowed the author's production of new books. But he remains active as president of Beginner Books and has plans for a number of new projects, such as Broadway musicals, new Beginner Books, and some video adaptations of his characters and stories to be used in educational software by Coleco. He works eight hours every day, ignoring any suggestions that he retire, working on two or three projects at a time. He remains a voracious reader, which may be one reason he keeps working and reworking his verse, so that it will measure up to the other examples of literature he reads; he admits to being unable to write in prose anymore. Though sometimes condemned in his later years for his moralizing, he says that the morals sometimes make their way into the stories as a result of the subject matter; he is never blatant, except perhaps in his political books. By his own count, there are only six "message books" out of forty-two which proves, he claims, that he is not really as overwhelmingly moralistic as critics have made him out to be.

He has never improved his drawing, but then he admits that he really cannot draw; so he simply capitalizes on his incapacity. "I've taken the awkwardness and peculiarities of my natural style and developed them." His style has become internationally recognizable; even without the Cat in the Hat logo on the cover of the Beginner Books, even very young children can recognize his two-dimensional style, with its loud, even garish, colors and thick, bold lines. One critic has claimed a family similarity among his characters, based on two features: "slightly batty, oval eyes and a smile you might find on the Mona Lisa after her first martini." His books reach an international audience because of their translation into such diverse languages as Polish and Maori, though the author maintains a particular fondness for those printed in braille. In spite of this international readership, the books remain particularly American: bright, even brash; optimistic, convinced of children's abilities to read and to reason; and encouraging of self-confidence, imagination, and appreciation of others.

Henry Kissinger, Statesman

Scott S. Smith

Henry Kissinger, along with his family, fled the Nazi regime and came to America at the age of fifteen, in 1938. He quickly adapted to his new home and joined the army during World War II. Kissinger's brilliant mind and easy way with people led him to prominence within American politics. As secretary of state in 1973, he was considered America's most admired man. In the following selection Scott S. Smith explains how Kissinger achieved his remarkable success. By combining his intelligence with his ability to endear himself to people in power, Kissinger became a skilled negotiator. Even today, now retired from politics, Kissinger is in great demand as a speaker and an authority on foreign policy. Scott S. Smith is a freelance writer.

Henry Kissinger was a very serious and brilliant young man. To many, he seemed arrogant. As his political career took off, the future German-born United States Secretary of State realized he had to change that impression if he wanted to win friends and influence people. He began using humor which was either self-deprecating or poked fun at his image.

He referred to his 1957 book *Nuclear Weapons and Foreign Policy* as "the most unread bestseller since (historian Arnold) Toynbee."

He announced to one audience that he had not faced

Scott S. Smith, "Henry Kissinger, Secrets of Success," *German Life*, vol. 8, September 30, 2001, p. 10. Copyright © 2001 by *German Life*. Reproduced by permission.

such a distinguished group since dining in a hall of mirrors.

Once, after flying off the handle with his staff he quipped that "since English is my second language, I didn't realize that 'maniac' and 'fool' were not terms of endearment."

When he was scheduled for a heart bypass operation, he remarked, "It proves that I do have a heart!"

Well Prepared for Political Life

Kissinger also found that a sharp wit combined with great conversational skills made him a popular guest at parties. He was able to talk to anyone because he had read widely, not just in his specialty of world history. At social events, he demonstrated his ability to get along with those with whom he had political differences. This was excellent training for getting along with world leaders whose personalities or policies he did not personally care for.

By 1973, Kissinger, the National Security Advisor (1969 to 1975) and Secretary of State (1973 to 1977), had an 85 percent public approval rating and was ranked by the Gallup Poll as America's most admired man, "the first and thus far only celebrity diplomat of the media age," comments Walter Isaacson in *Kissinger: A Biography.*

With his portly figure and professorial look, he was an improbable "sex symbol," as he was by this time portrayed. However, Kissinger was not simply indulging his ego in cultivating the media—he knew that fame gave him more leverage in working towards his political goals.

It was quite an achievement for the boy born Heinz Alfred Kissinger in Bavaria in 1923 to Orthodox Jewish parents. His family fled Nazi persecution in 1938, settling in New York City.

Those childhood experiences caused him to be distrustful of everyone and to learn to never show weakness, personally or in his work.

Kissinger learned early on that one way to be successful was to be a careful observer of others. When he joined
the United States Army in 1943, he wrote his brother, who
was planning to sign up, to go in "with your eyes and your
ears open and your mouth closed." This approach to learning led Henry to be named administrator of regions in
post-war Germany where he had virtually dictatorial pow-
ers. It was an extraordinary executive experience from age
22 to 24.

Honing His People Skills

In and out of the Army, Kissinger discovered another path
to success: flattery. He found that no matter how much
power someone had or however much money the individ-
ual made, everyone loved to receive praise. He began to
perfect the art of giving it, endearing himself to people in
high places.

His patrons included everyone from Nelson Rockefeller,
the New York governor and later Vice President, to Hamilton Fish Armstrong, editor of *Foreign Affairs*, who got
him a position on the Council on Foreign Affairs, where
Kissinger could rub shoulders with world leaders.

Kissinger also developed personal bonds that were useful during his career climb by sharing supposed confi-
dences, telling someone he or she was the only one who
would fully appreciate the information.

Kissinger built relationships in another way: by playing
off enemies against each other, acting as a confidant to
each and commenting disparagingly about the opponent.
Classmates at Harvard were amazed when he managed to
befriend two professors who hated each other. He later
took this to the geo-political level in forging relationships
with officials in China and the Soviet Union based on their
mutual distrust.

This required keeping the big picture in mind, mastering details and being able to analyze how one action would affect the whole. These related traits were, commented President Richard Nixon, his greatest strengths as a diplomat.

A Great Political Mind

Nixon also noted that Kissinger's success was in part due to his understanding of how government bureaucracy worked, so that he could make moves in favor of or against individuals according to his personal interests. Kissinger usually succeeded in getting what he wanted.

However, he did not waste time on bureaucratic battles unless he thought something significant was involved in the long run. He disdained the turf fights in academia as so bitter "because the stakes were so small."

Kissinger was able to achieve results because he was committed to what he saw as Realpolitik: realism in politics. Idealism was for the naïve, he felt, and it often ended in greater tragedy than a less high-minded, but more practical approach.

Secrecy became one of the trademarks of Kissinger's method of operating and it often proved useful during his years in the White House, ranging from three years of talks in Paris with representatives of North Vietnam to his trip to China to prepare for the visit of President Nixon.

There had been 134 sessions between United States and Chinese ambassadors in Warsaw trying to narrow differences between 1954 and 1968, when they recessed for a year for lack of a single agreement. Nixon and Kissinger realized that the State Department bureaucracy would have to end-run to accomplish anything, since too many officials were opposed to diplomatic relations with China.

The breakthrough began with Kissinger's visit to Beijing in July 1971, where he established an immediate rapport with Premier Zhou Enlai, a fellow intellectual.

Kissinger's strength as a negotiator with sides who

seemed to be far apart was due to his ability to "fudge and feint and find ways to concede points that didn't matter while obscuring a few that did," observes Isaacson. He could find the right words that each side would interpret as reflecting its interests.

Once an agreement was reached, Kissinger understood the importance of being dramatic to capture attention and have a platform to explain why this was a positive development.

To build political support for his actions, Kissinger learned other elements of public relations. To insure that his views were conveyed, he attempted to influence White House speechwriters for President Nixon and President Gerald Ford.

Once he became known worldwide after the breakthrough with China, Kissinger began to make speeches himself to shape public opinion.

Most important, be cultivated relationships with political reporters and commentators. When he arrived at his office each morning, he would first return the calls of journalists.

Nor was he content with simply talking to those who agreed with him. He spent considerable time trying to bring around even his harshest critics to his point of view. His memoirs (*White House Years, Years of Upheaval, Years of Renewal*) continued that effort.

Heidi Klum, Supermodel

Sara Vilkomerson

In the following selection Sara Vilkomerson describes su-
permodel Heidi Klum's business sense and relentless work
ethic, two traits that have kept her in the spotlight long after her days on the fashion runway ended. The author tells
of how Klum's early years in Germany helped shape her
drive to succeed and how her subsequent success in the
United States has been modeled on the example her hard-
working father set for her. Vilkomerson is a writer for the
New York Observer.

Inside a pristine tent in Bryant Park [New York], the
German-born swimsuit model turned international marketing phenom Heidi Klum was gleaming coolly under a
blitzkrieg of flashing lights, clad in a low-cut Donna Karan
silver tank top that hugged her impossible curves. It was
the grand finale of her weirdly addictive Bravo reality
show, *Project Runway,* and the place, which smelled like
new car, was packed. The front row included a newly
slimmed down, bestubbled Harvey Weinstein (who, along
with Ms. Klum, serves as an executive producer), the entire cast of *Queer Eye for the Straight Guy* and stentorian
Inside the Actors Studio host James Lipton, all there to
cheer their network's newest star.

A few days earlier, Ms. Klum (pronounced Kloom) appeared a bit more mercifully mortal, padding about her

management company's downtown office in a red zip-up pullover and jeans. "I think the windows are a little grimy," she said, eyes narrowing. "I guess I try to be a perfection-ist. I look at things and the first thing I think of is, 'How can I change this? How can I make this better?'"

Ambitious Ventures

Welcome to Heidi, Inc. As she closes in on 32, an age when models used to be lucky to get wrinkle-cream endorse-ments, Ms. Klum is hard at work perfecting her own per-sonal brand, as we all must these days, into perpetuity. There's an eponymous fragrance (of course), a footwear line with Birkenstock, an autobiography suggesting Niet-zschean aphorisms (Body of Knowledge: 8 Rules of Model Behavior; Crown), three types of candy (one is flavored with yogurt, befitting her wholesome Germanic image) and clothing, jewelry and endorsement deals that run the gamut from Liz Claiborne to McDonald's.

"She is, in this hyphenated world, one of the few people who really deserve all the hyphens," said the designer and Upper East Side favorite Michael Kors, one of *Project Runway*'s more incongruous judges.

The show, a sort of *American Idol* for the fashion world, has emerged as one of reality TV's biggest hits this season [2005]. It premiered to modest ratings on Dec. 1, 2004, but has been picking up viewers like lint tape ever since. The Feb. 2 episode, which revolved around the final five contestants revamping a postal-service uniform, brought in the highest numbers in Bravo's history for the Wednesday 9 P.M. time slot. "I have a personal interest in making a great show," Ms. Klum said, flashing her shiny teeth.

"Under the smiles, under all that blond fluff," said her former agent John Casablancas on the phone later, "there is a heart of a shark."

A Well-Developed Work Ethic

The younger of two children, Heidi Klum was born and raised in the small town of Bergisch-Gladbach, outside Cologne, as in the original Eau de, "this perfume that seriously every household in Germany has in their closet," she said. "People use it as a stain remover."

Her mother was a hair stylist and her father was a "high-up" executive at the massive 4711 cosmetics company in Germany. Heidi completed the national mandatory youth internship at her father's company, where she learned about class differences. "He wanted me to see the range of work," she said. "When I was down on the conveyor belt he said, 'Don't make any jokes, Heidi, and don't talk down to anyone.' Not that I would be mean or anything," she hastened to explain. "But he just wanted to be sure that I wasn't going to say anything like 'This is so stupid' or 'This is so boring' or 'Why do I have to wear a hair net?'"

Herr Klum also imparted a work ethic. "My father was always early out of the house and coming home late," she said. "I saw that in order to make money, we didn't have a lot, but we did do things like go on holiday, I understood it was because my father worked so hard."

Taking an early interest in fashion, she was accepted to design school in Dusseldorf at 18. Then, one day, she and a girlfriend were flipping through a magazine and saw an advertisement for a national modeling contest. They sent in Polaroids on a lark. Five months later, Ms. Klum got a call from the contest's producers.

Embarking on a Modeling Career

She beat out 30,000 other girls to become Ms. Model 1992. "I looked around at these other girls, and I started to think, 'What can I do next?'" Ms. Klum said. "My father was not too excited about it. He didn't believe in me having all that good a look. I mean, I'm sure he thought his daughter was pretty, but I don't think he ever thought I could win this big competition and really make it. To him, I was his daughter with the pimples and problems going to parties with my friends."

The International Metropolitan Agency signed her immediately and sent her packing to Paris and Milan. But remember, this was 1992. Heroin chic and the waifish Kate Moss were ascendant. The more sturdily built Ms. Klum was not in vogue. "I had big boobs and curvy hips," she writes in her book. "The agency started coaching me on my appearance. . . . There was that special 'mix': 'Mix this with that and drink it so you'll lose weight,' they urged. They also stripped me down and weighed and measured me, keeping rigorous records. I felt like a piece of meat. I wasn't going to drink that water and I refused to show up at parties populated with guys who expected me to sleep with them."

Frustrated, Ms. Klum called Metropolitan's New York office. They sent her to cheesy Miami. Within days, her passport was stolen. She got sick of hotel lobbies swarming with models and begged for a chance in the Northeast.

Determined and Dedicated

For three months she went on "go-sees," only to slink . . . home to the squalid apartment on 18th Street that she shared with two roommates. The work she was getting was strictly catalog: J.C. Penney, Chadwick's, Newport News. Ms. Klum switched agencies to Elite, then owned by Mr. Casablancas. "The early Heidi days were a delight," he said. Though he once referred to the model as a "talentless German sausage" in a 2000 article (after she left him for her current management, IMG), he seems to have mellowed since. "She was a young full-of-life model who had paid her dues as a catalog model for a few years, and then we started bringing her to the next level. I personally keep excellent memories of her. She's very dedicated, she's very German in her way of being concentrated on the ultimate goal."

Ms. Klum disagrees that that drive is a national trait of the Vaterland [Fatherland—that is, Germany]. "My very best girlfriend who is also German is the exact opposite of me!" she exclaimed. "She sat on my couch for three months and she did not have the drive or the ambition to be a photographer's assistant."

She said that Elite initially resisted her idea to be shopped to Victoria's Secret. "You can't wait for things to come to you, especially in this business," she said.

Before you could say "garter belt," she was suddenly the newest hottie alongside [models] Stephanie Seymour and Claudia Schiffer. "She's imposed a look that's somewhere between a Pamela Anderson and a top model," Mr. Casablancas said. "She's just in between, and she's been able to give the sexy blonde a nobility."

Booked on the *Late Show* with David Letterman, she showed up in a black, open-sided, barely there Marc Bouwer dress akin to the one that made [model] Elizabeth Hurley's career. Heidi played the good sport, enthusiastically yodeling for Dave.

A tape of the episode found its way to Elaine D'Farley, then the editor of *Sports Illustrated*'s [*SI*] swimsuit edition, "I saw her portfolio and it was weak," said Ms. D'Farley, now the beauty director of *Self*. "But she was so charming and down-to-earth in person, I thought even without the pedigrees that some of the other girls had, with that personality we'd be able to get some great pictures from her."

Ms. Klum ended up on the cover, her bounteous cleavage spilling from her one-piece like ripe fruit.

"She was so smart about it," Ms. D'Farley said. "While we were doing the issue she said, 'I need a publicist.' She's constantly aligning herself with a team of people that can support her and bring her to the next level."

Minor Setbacks

Ms. Klum alleges she was actually quite naive in the early years of her stardom. "I had no idea when a contract was put under my nose, it could have been Chinese," she said. "You start asking a lot of questions and people don't like it. People think that when you're nice that you aren't capable of doing different things, or they take you for granted and want to step all over you. There's so many people that want a piece of the pie. It's like if someone sneezed in a same room when something happened, they're like, 'Oh, remember me? I'm the one who sneezed.'"

One sneeze in Ms. Klum's life was her 1997 marriage to Ric Pipino, a hairdresser. They separated five years later. Mr. Pipino gets a few platitudes in her book, but Ms. Klum refused to elaborate on those years to *The Observer*. (Likewise Mr. Pipino, whose P.R. rep said he "had nothing but warm and good feelings for Heidi but will not comment on her.")

"He was bad news," Mr. Casablancas said simply.

After the marriage was over, Ms. Klum was dragged through the tabloids when she became pregnant by Renault Formula 1 boss Flavio Briatore, who left her six months later. But things have quieted down. She is now raising her eight-month [old] daughter, Leni, with the British pop singer Seal, who proposed marriage on a glacier the day before Christmas Eve. The couple has homes in London, Los Angeles and the West Village. "The good thing about having a partner that is famous is that he understands it," Ms. Klum said. "I think it makes it easier."

From Suzy Parker on, it used to be that models would hop right off the runways into a casting office, or perhaps to start a cosmetics line. Then came Cindy Crawford, who became the world's top-paid model over a decade ago thanks to deals with Pepsi, Kay Jewelers and Revlon. She hosted House of Style on MTV and produced a line of exercise videos through a production company, Crawdaddy Inc.

Ms. Klum has done a few movie cameos and appeared on episodes of *Spin City*, but has no intention of pursuing an acting career, perhaps learning from her predecessor's notorious turn in *Fair Game*. "I think that is something you are either born with, or you go and learn," she said. "And I don't feel like I'm born with that talent."

Going strictly by the numbers, the most successful swimsuit model turned mogul is not Ms. Crawford, but Kathy Ireland, whose company grossed $1 billion [in 2004]. Kathy Ireland Worldwide sells products from window treatments to towels to socks, branded with the heavy-browed former *SI* model's name and/or image at 34,000 different locations in 14 countries.

Ms. Klum worries if she got that big, there might be a quality-control issue.

"Kathy Ireland is huge," she said. "She's very mass, which is great, but I was never ready to go in that direction. I think it would be hard to oversee everything and I don't like things to just slip through my hands."

Of course, with a German clothing line ("It's swimsuits, it's jeans, it's all the things that I love; I just finished doing some bomber jackets and fur"), a jewelry line with Mouawad at Saks (first-year revenue: $20 million) and those Birkenstocks (she designed a special pair for Bill Clinton), there might be some concern about diluting the brand.

But Ms. Klum insists it's as strong as Eau de Cologne.

"For me, its about having control of my image," she said. "I like to do everything myself. If I put my stamp on something, then I want it to have come through my hands first."

And who needs New York Fashion Week? She was getting ready for a trip back to her native land, where she and the rest of the Klum family were planning to dress as green dragons and throw five tons of her candy off their float for Carnival. "You know how we are in Germany," she said. "If it's made in Germany, we're very proud of that. I'm a little bit like that too."

CHRONOLOGY

1608

Several Germans are among the original settlers of Jamestown, the first American settlement.

1626

Peter Minuit, who was born in Germany but resettled in Holland, arrives in New Amsterdam (later New York) to serve as governor of the colony.

1683

Thirteen German Mennonite families arrive in Pennsylvania and establish Germantown, just outside Philadelphia.

1688

Four prominent residents of Germantown, including Daniel Francis Pastorius, write the first protest against slavery.

1732

In Philadelphia, the first German-language newspaper, *Philadelphische Zeitung*, is published.

1733

John Peter Zenger, a redemptioner from the Palatine region of Germany, founds a newspaper called the *New-York Weekly Journal* to voice opposition to the policies of New York's colonial governor, William Cosby.

1735

Zenger is acquitted of seditious libel in a landmark victory for freedom of the press.

1743

Christopher Saur, a printer living in Philadelphia, prints the first European-language Bible in America—in German.

1772

Germans from Pennsylvania (the "Dutchmen") form their own militias during the buildup to the Revolutionary War.

1778

General Friedrich Wilhelm von Steuben, an expert in training troops, is persuaded to come to America to lend his military expertise to the American revolutionists.

1784

John Jacob Astor arrives in America. He establishes a fur-trading business and becomes the wealthiest man in the country.

1790

German immigrants comprise 8.6 percent of the population of the United States. In Pennsylvania their population is estimated to be 33 percent.

1805

Religious leader George Rapp and his "Harmonist" followers, separatists from the German Lutheran Church, found a utopian society in Harmony, Pennsylvania. They later found New Harmony on thirty thousand acres of land in Indiana.

1821

The German custom of decorating a tree at Christmas is introduced to the United States by the Pennsylvania Dutch in Lancaster, Pennsylvania.

1823

The first German singing society, or *Liederverein*, is founded in Cincinnati.

1825

The Harmonists build their third town, Economy, twenty miles northwest of Pittsburgh.

1829

In Germany, Gottfried Duden publishes an account of his blissful three years in Missouri, which encourages thousands of Germans to immigrate to the area.

1845

A group of German aristocrats, led by Prince Carl of Solms-Braunfels, bring 150 families to settle in Texas, establishing the town of New Braunfels, Texas.

1848–1849

The failure of the democratic revolution in Germany causes thousands of "Forty-Eighters" to immigrate and settle in the United States.

1850s

Nearly 1 million Germans arrive during this peak immigration period. More than two hundred thousand immigrate in 1854 alone.

1856

Margaretha Schurz, wife of Civil War general Carl Schurz, establishes the first American kindergarten in Watertown, Wisconsin.

1857

Adolphus Busch settles in St. Louis, Missouri. He later marries the daughter of a brewer and begins what would become the Anheuser-Busch Brewing Association.

1861–1865

More than five thousand German immigrants volunteer for the Union Army during the Civil War.

1877

Civil War general Carl Schurz becomes secretary of the interior.

1880s

During this period, the decade of the highest number of German immigrants, approximately 1.5 million Germans settle in the United States.

1886

The Haymarket labor riots in Chicago lead to the arrest, conviction, and execution of several German Americans.

1910

An estimated 2.3 million German Americans now reside in the United States.

1917

The United States enters World War I, triggering anti-German hysteria throughout the country.

1920

Prohibition begins, obliterating the brewery businesses of many German Americans.

1933

Adolf Hitler comes to power in Germany, creating a brain drain of 130,000 artists and intellectuals, who flee to the United States.

1937

The American Nazi Party claims approximately two hundred thousand members.

1948

The Displaced Persons Act is established to provide for the immigration of displaced persons in Eastern Europe, including ethnic Germans, to the United States.

1952

More than eighty thousand post-Holocaust German Jews have immigrated to America. Dwight D. Eisenhower, a German American, is elected president of the United States.

1968

The society for German American Studies is founded to study the history, culture, folklore, genealogy, language, literature, and creative arts of Germans in North America.

1973

German-born Henry Kissinger becomes secretary of state and receives the Nobel Peace Prize.

1990

The U.S. census determines that German Americans are the largest ethnic group in America.

2000

The 2000 U.S. census reveals that 43 million Americans, or 15 percent of the population, claim German ancestry.

General Histories of German Immigration

F.W. Bogen, *The German Immigrant in America*. Ed. Don Heinrich Tolzmann. Bowie, MD: Heritage, 1992.

John Archibald Bole, *The Harmony Society: A Chapter in German American Culture History*. New York: AMS, 1973.

Frank R. Diffenderfer, *The German Immigration into Pennsylvania Through the Port of Philadelphia from 1700 to 1775 and the Redemptioners*. Baltimore: Genealogical, 1977.

Johannes Gilhoff, *Letters of a German American Farmer: Jurnjakob Swehn Travels to America*. Trans. Richard Trost. Iowa City: University of Iowa Press, 2000.

Theodore Gish and Richard Spuler, eds., *Eagle in the New World: German Immigration to Texas and America*. College Station: Texas A&M University Press, 1986.

James E. Haas, *Conrad Poppenhusen: The Life of a German-American Industrial Pioneer*. Baltimore: Gateway, 2004.

Don Heinrich Tolzmann, *German-American Studies: Selected Essays*. New York: Peter Lang, 2001.

Frank Trommler and Joseph McVeigh, eds., *America and the Germans: An Assessment of a Three-Hundred Year History*. Philadelphia: University of Pennsylvania Press, 1985.

Joseph Wandel, *The German Dimension of American History*. Chicago: Nelson-Hall, 1979.

Stephanie Grauman Wolf, *Urban Village: Population,*

Community, and Family Structure in Germantown, Pennsylvania, 1683–1800. Princeton, NJ: Princeton University Press, 1976.

German Americans and U.S. Wars

Joseph Berger, *Displaced Persons: Growing Up American After the Holocaust*. New York: Scribner, 2001.

Robert H. Ferrell, *Woodrow Wilson and World War I, 1917–1921*. New York: Harper & Row, 1985.

Stephen Fox, *America's Invisible Gulag: A Biography of German American Internment & Exclusion in World War II: Memory and History*. New York: Peter Lang, 2000.

Timothy J. Holian, *The German-Americans and World War II: An Ethnic Experience*. New York: Peter Lang, 1996.

Arthur D. Jacobs, *The Prison Called Hohenasperg: An American Boy Betrayed by His Government During World War II*. Boca Raton, FL: Universal, 1999.

Wilhelm Kaufman, *The Germans in the American Civil War: With a Biographical Directory*. Ed. Don Heinrich Tolzmann. Trans. Steven Rowan. Carlisle, PA: John Kallmann, 1999.

Phyllis Keller, *States of Belonging: German-American Intellectuals and the First World War*. Cambridge, MA: Harvard University Press, 1979.

Bruce Levine, *The Spirit of 1848: German Immigrants, Labor Conflict, and the Coming of the Civil War*. Urbana: University of Illinois Press, 1992.

Don Heinrich Tolzmann, ed., *German-Americans in the American Revolution: Henry Melchior Muhlenberg Richards' History*. Bowie, MD: Heritage, 1992.

Hans L. Trefousse, *Carl Schurz: A Biography*. New York: Fordham University Press, 1998.

Lewis E. Unnewehr, *Silent Night, Unholy Night: The Story of German-Americans During World War I.* New York: Vantage, 2000.

German American Culture and Assimilation

David W. Detjen, *The Germans in Missouri, 1900–1918: Prohibition, Neutrality, and Assimilation.* Columbia: University of Missouri Press, 1985.

Ursula Hegi, *Tearing the Silence: Being German in America.* New York: Simon & Schuster, 1997.

Dorothy Hoobler and Thomas Hoobler, *The German American Family Album.* New York: Oxford University Press, 1996.

Russell A. Kazal, *Becoming Old Stock: The Paradox of German-American Identity.* Princeton, NJ: Princeton University Press, 2004.

Helmut Keil, ed., *German Workers' Culture in the United States, 1850 to 1920.* Washington, DC: Smithsonian Institution, 1988.

Joachim Liebschner, *A Child's Work: Freedom and Play in Froebel's Educational Theory and Practice.* New York: Lutterworth, 2002.

Peter C. Merrill, *German Immigrant Artists in America: A Biographical Dictionary.* Lanham, MD: Scarecrow, 1997.

Herman W. Ronnenberg, *Beer and Brewing in the Inland Northwest, 1850 to 1950.* Moscow: University of Idaho Press, 1993.

———, *The Politics of Assimilation: The Effect of Prohibition on the German-Americans.* New York: Carlton, 1975.

Don Heinrich Tolzmann, *German-American Achievements: 400 Years of Contributions to America.* Westminster, MD: Heritage, 2001.

Frank Trommler and Elliott Shore, eds., *The German-American Encounter: Conflict and Cooperation Between Two Cultures, 1800–2000*. New York: Berghahn, 2001.

John D. Zug and Karen Gottier, eds., *German American Life: Recipes and Traditions*. Iowa City, IA: Penfield, 1991.

Web Sites

Freedom of Information Times, www.foitimes.com/intern ment/index.html. This Web site contains research materials and personal accounts of the treatment of Americans of German ancestry during World War II.

German Corner, www.germancorner.com. Calendars of festivals, discussion groups, recipes, and general information, all relating to German American culture, can be found on this Web site.

German Embassy, Washington, D.C., www.germany-info. org/relaunch/culture/ger_americans/paper.html. The German Embassy's Web site provides comprehensive information about German American history, culture, news, education, business, and technology.

Max Kade German American Center/Society for German American Studies, www-lib.iupui.edu/kade/home. html. Maintained by Indiana University–Purdue University, Indianapolis, this Web site is a research center for German American studies.

INDEX

220 The Germans

culture, 10–17, 57, 68–76, 79
    American, 104–106, 108–11
    preservation of, 99, 112–14,
        127, 159, 161–65
    religion and, 47, 50–54
Czechoslovakia, 165

dancing, 14, 79
Daniels, Roger, 56
Davis, Jacob, 167, 171–74
Delaware, Lord, 35
deli, 18
Democrats, 160
Dickstein-McCormack
    Congressional Investigatory
    Committee, 124–26
discrimination. See Jews,
    discrimination against;
    prejudice
displaced persons, 159
    see also exiles; Holocaust,
        survivors of
Doerries, Reinhard R., 45
draft, military, 98–101, 131–32
Dutch. See German Americans

Easter, 12–13
economics, 56–61, 79, 162
    see also prosperity
education, 19–21, 72–73, 78, 148
    religious, 45, 52–54, 80
Ehret, George, 86
Einstein, Albert, 178–85
Einstein, Eduard, 179
Einstein, Elsa, 180
Einstein, Hans Albert, 179
Einstein, Hermann, 178
Einstein, Mileva Maric, 179
Eisenhower, Dwight D., 60,
    159–60
elections, 62–63, 159–60
electromagnetism, 183
England/English, 11, 24–36, 51,
    60
English (language), 47, 54, 102

Europe, 46–48, 50–51, 59
    see also individual countries
Evans, Harold, 167
exiles, 103–14, 135–46

festivals, 10–15, 79, 162
Feuchtwanger, Lion, 103–104,
    109–10
Feuchtwanger, Marta, 103–104,
    113
films, 107–108
First Amendment
    (Constitution), 49
Fisher, Johann Anton, 72–73
foods, 10, 15–17, 19
Forty-eighters, 59–60, 164
Fox, George, 38
Frank, Bruno, 109
Frankfurt Company, 39
frankfurters, 16
Franz (carpenter), 25, 28–35
Freethinkers, 45–46, 48, 54
Friends of German Democracy,
    95
Friends of New Germany, 118,
    120–27
Froebel, Friedrich, 20
Fuhr, Eberhard E., 128

Gaulle, Charles de, 165
Gau-USA, 119–20
Gebhart, William, 16
Geisel, Helen Palmer, 190–91,
    194, 196
Geisel, Henrietta Seuss, 186,
    188, 190
Geisel, Theodor Robert, 186–89
Geisel, Theodor Seuss, 186–97
gemütlichkeit, 88
German (language), 54, 101, 163
German-American Bund, 118
German American Day, 21, 40
German Americans, 21
    arrival of, 24–36
    identity as, 158–65